EFFECTIVE COMMUNICATION IN THE WORKPLACE

A Practical Guide to Improve Interpersonal Communication in the Workplace for Better Environment, Client Relationships, and Employee Engagement

Table of Contents

Introduction

Thank you for purchasing this book. It is my pleasure to give you a starting point and blueprint on how to communicate with others effectively in the workplace and in any organization.

We communicate with each other all the time verbally or non-verbally, yet we rarely think about it. We often communicate without being fully aware of the messages we are really sending to people. Communicating effectively depends on being understood, listening to others and listening with empathy.

EFFECTIVE COMMUNICATION IN THE WORKPLACE

Good communication is an important skill in any environment, organization with human interactions. Moreover, when it comes to communication in the business, effective communication is an integral element to business success.

In any organization, good communication isn't just about resolving conflicts. Good communication is an important element in client relationships, profitability, team effectiveness, and employee engagement.

Building healthy working relationships is vital to any business success. A major part of this is understanding your own personal communication style, how you can influence other people, and how to use your communication style to create effective business relationships and it isn't just about being able to more accurately speak and concisely present your thought and ideas. It's also not just about resolving conflict or creating a more positive team environment.

Communication is essential to sales, client relationships, a better team environment, company culture, and employee and team management engagement.

Communication skills, like anything else, can be developed and improved with practice and with proper education. Improve your communication skills in writing, interpersonal conversations, presentations, interviews, and more by reading this book.

Learn to write more effectively, communicate with customers and employees, and craft compelling communication plans and proposals, as well as communication skills training for difficult situations, such as dealing and managing.

Chapter 1: What is Effective Workplace Communication?

Perhaps one of the reasons that effective communication in the workplace is being taken for granted in some workplaces is because some people don't really know what it means. What is effective workplace communication, anyway?

Today, advanced technology has made it possible for

communication in the office to be done without the need for face-to-face communication. Bosses just send emails to the managers and the managers do the same to the supervisors. The supervisors then just relay important updates to the employees through text messages, Skype chat or some other form of digital communication. In the past, when there was important news to be shared with the workers of a company, upper management would call for a meeting with middle management and middle management would have a meeting with the workers afterward. These days, however, there just isn't time to hold traditional meetings. The speed at which businesses move prevents people from connecting on a personal level, and people have learned to sacrifice face-to-face communication for faster business transactions. Meetings are done through Skype chats and people no longer need to travel or be physically present for a conference. And while modern means of communication have their own merits, the quality of communication in the workplace may be suffering. Because of the lack of opportunities to connect on a personal level, communication barriers arise, causing communication problems between the employer and employees, and also between the workers themselves.

In order to have effective workplace communication, people should be able to connect on a personal level. There should be opportunities for face-to-face interaction so that communication barriers can be minimized or removed. When people don't communicate face-to-face, they cannot observe the facial expressions, voice, pitch and body language of the people with whom they are communicating.

For instance, managers, supervisors and people in middle management positions must also possess good communication skills. They should be courteous when talking with other employees because, when it comes to courtesy in a workplace, position should not be an issue at all. All people in the company, whether boss or employee, must make an effort to speak and behave in a polite or courteous manner when communicating with each other.

All communications must be clear and concise so as to minimize any chance for misunderstandings. Words must be chosen carefully when relaying important messages and, in case there are misunderstandings, there should always be an opportunity for clarifications. Jargon should not be used when communicating with people outside one's own department because that will only alienate other workers and cause communication barriers. Studies also prove that men and women in the workplace communicate differently. Men, in general, will use fewer words and gestures than women when communicating. People in the workplace must also be sensitive to race and culture in order to have more effective communication in the workplace.

Chapter 2: Internal Workplace Communication

In day to day business, we exchange a lot of emails with our team(s), cross-functional teams and other business entities. In the global business landscape, the internal group or business unit plays the role of a stakeholder if a segment of their work is handled by another team for their customer. Hence, it is important to pay attention to internal communication as we would do with external customers/clients. Most often, email exchanges within teams are semi-formal or informal in nature. This approach works as long as the email trail remains within the team and the same conversation thread is not extended or forwarded to customers.

Meeting Etiquette

Some of these points have been discussed earlier in this book. To make it specific to the context of internal communication, here are some good practices that will help you professionally conduct meetings:

• The agenda is the most important content of a meeting.

• The organizer must ensure that the invitees are informed of their role in the meeting.

• It may not be possible to discuss all the points on the agenda at times. The organizer must ensure that the meeting objective is met. If more time is required to dwell on the subject, another follow-up meeting is a good option.

• The organizer must send out the minutes of the meeting highlighting the action item, owner, and due date. This needs to be tracked and updated to the entire team until all the open items are concluded.

• At times, we may not pay the same attention to an internal meeting compared to a customer meeting. This will impact the quality of the discussion and eventually may hamper customer satisfaction as the internal meetings are directed towards meeting the customer's objectives.

Email Etiquette

While drafting quick notes or emails for circulation within the teams, here are a few important points to keep in mind which will help align the team to work on a common goal. Remember, people always observe what we say and what we do.

• Before sending an email, do a quick check on the "To" and "CC" list and make sure that only those who need to take action are in the "To" list and those who need to be informed are in the "CC" list.

• Before replying to an email, make sure whether all recipients need to be included in the ongoing discussion. Use "Reply All" and "Reply" with discretion.

• Using "BCC" is not a good practice as it hides the information from other recipients. If there is a need to do a "BCC" to a large group, mention in your email about it.

• At times, a discussion thread may turn into an argument when people are exchanging their views. If you are party to that, have a direct, one-to-one conversation with the other person instead of discussing issues in an open forum. The rest of the team can be appraised of the outcome of your discussion.

• If you are forwarding the status update from your team to a customer/stakeholder, do a quick check of the body of the message. Scroll through the message body to ensure it contains relevant points that can be shared in a common forum.

Chapter 3: External Workplace Communication

External communication can be with the external world (market, business world, etc.) or with external clients and stakeholders. In the context of this discussion, the audience for external communication is clients and other stakeholders who need to be informed of the progress of the project/program.

Sufficient care needs to be taken to handle such communication as they can impact the business outcome with clients or stakeholders directly. External communication has enormous power in enabling customer success. It is a powerful tool to show our passion and commitment to clients. Every organization aims to become a Trusted Advisor to their clients hence external communication plays a crucial role in developing customer relationships. As said in the beginning, everything we do is communication, and the rest of the world understands our motives/intentions through what we say, write and do.

The corporate communications team releases certain business-specific communication with appropriate titles such as "confidential," "for internal circulation only," "for internal and external audience" and so on. As an employee, you may be entitled to receive key business updates before it is released to the external world. It is important to use your discretion in forwarding such communication to various groups as they may be subject to strict business conduct laws by the organization. This applies to a project-specific communication sent by customers. Any customer sensitive data/communication should be secured at all times without compromising data integrity.

Communication is our face to the external world. We also keep having inner dialogues with our self which shapes our outer personality. Small things that make a big difference in the professional setup (based on my experience):

• Accept the meeting invite to let the speaker know your availability.
• If you are in a noisy place when you join the teleconference, let the organizer know about it and mute your line until you get your turn to speak.
• Plan well to reach the meeting venue on time. On the day of the meeting, the car breaks down, the bus arrives late and every other reason supports why we are late, but it does not give a good impression to the speaker/organizer.
• Avoid the temptation to give your opinion without consent when others are in a conversation.

- Be sensitive towards personal space, cultural practices and differences.
- Avoid the temptation to chat and do cross-talks when the session is in progress.
- If you have joined a webinar, do not leave your desk after entering the webinar. The organizer may not be able to see if you are around and this is unprofessional behavior.
- If you need to help your colleague during meeting/presentations, be transparent about it.
- Avoid the presence of others in the meeting without informing the host.
- "YES" is an equally powerful opposite to "NO"... which can be used effectively. Say "No" when you cannot achieve or complete something in a short duration. It is better to say "No" upfront rather than failing after committing to complete it.

Chapter 4: Group Workplace Communication

At a business unit level, most companies may not have the luxury of having a specific marketing team handling group communication as the team mostly caters to companywide communication and announcements. To make sure that the teams are aligned with the company's objectives, timely communication from the senior management or leadership team plays a key role here. This could be in virtual, written form or through town hall meetings. Group communication may also involve external parties (based on the business context) and other members.

Group communication is the voice of the business unit to its team. They get to know how the business is functioning and the alignment of each project/program to meet the organization's objective.

Webinars/virtual meetings

Webinars or virtual meetings are used to reach a larger audience across different geographical locations. These are also one of the effective ways to manage virtual communication, training, and conference/meetings with customers. The organizer will be dealing with a large number of participants in webinars. Hence, it needs to be managed effectively to ensure the communication objectives are met. Some tips to ensure a smooth experience during webinars:

• As an organizer, set the ground rules before the webinar begins.

• It is a good practice to test the bridge before the webinar begins as technical glitches can catch you by surprise any time.

• Introduce the topic and the speaker, then announce how the questions will be handled.

• Mute the lines of all participants to avoid interference of external noise.

• Facilitate questions between the participant and the speaker.

• If there are additional questions and the session time is getting extended, make a note of those questions and ensure that they are answered by the speaker through emails.

Chapter 5: How to Communicate Effectively at Work

If there was ever a place where communication skills mattered the most, it is in the workplace. If you can master the ability to communicate effectively with not just your colleagues, but your superiors, managers and all staff levels in every industry, you are in a position of power because you hold one of the most valuable skills an employee can possess.

Even though we live in a digital age where the majority of our work is conducted online, over the phones, through emails or even through social media (as a lot of companies tend to do their marketing these days), effective communication skills are still a prized asset that is not going to go away anytime soon.

At work, we are required to communicate a lot more than we normally would in our everyday lives. We're communicating with clients, with colleagues, with managers, with bosses, through emails, over the phone and even during meetings and presentations. Here is what you can do to improve your communication skills at the workplace:

Improve Your Body Language – Body language is applicable in the workplace too, perhaps even more so because this is where it really matters. At work, the way you carry yourself and communicate is just as important as how well you get the job done. Remember how our nonverbal cues can speak volumes even when we don't say a word? So, while at work, always adopt confident body language whenever you step into your workplace. Do not slouch, do not fold or cross your arms, do not frown or look sullen. Always be positive, and project a warm and welcoming manner, smile and make eye contact with the people you pass by.

Avoid Over-Communicating – Avoid being long-winded and beating around the bush when you have discussions and conversations at work. You may think you are trying to be as effective as possible by communicating every little detail, even what is seemingly unnecessary, but avoid doing that because there is such a thing as over-communicating. Even in presentations, droning on for too long puts you at risk of losing the attention span of your audience. The best way to communicate effectively is to be brief, concise and only communicate what is necessary and relevant to the situation or discussion at hand.

Seek Feedback – The best way to know if you are effective in what you do, or if what you are doing is working, is to seek feedback, honest feedback from your colleagues. Regularly seeking feedback will help you discover what areas you should be working on to improve, and often it is others who can shed better perspective on the things that we may overlook.

Engage with Your Audience – If you are tasked with presenting at a meeting, this is a great way for you to put into practice your effective communication skills. Now, business presentations are not the most riveting topic, and attention spans will drift eventually, so what do effective communicators do? They engage with their audience. Being effective in your communication requires that you can deliver the points you want to say to an audience that is paying attention. During the meeting or presentation, ask questions and encourage your audience to respond and share their points of view.

Watching Your Tone of Voice – At the workplace, you need to always ensure that your tone is professional yet friendly and welcoming at the same time. Sometimes it may be necessary to be assertive to stand firm on a point, but still, try and maintain a professional tone when you do that to avoid coming off as aggressive. Effective communication at work requires that you be able to master being confident, direct, professional yet calm and cooperative at the same time.

Checking Your Grammar – This step is applicable for emails and written communication at the workplace. The most effective communicators are ones who can write flawlessly with no mistakes because they put in the extra effort to check and proofread everything that they type or write before they hit the send button. Check it twice, check it thrice, and check it as many times as you need to ensure everything is completely on point before it gets sent. You will impress everyone with your perfect grammar and punctuation, and the ones who read your emails will be able to understand what you are trying to say just as if you were standing there in front of them talking to them.

Listening Well – Listening makes an appearance here again, because communication, as previously mentioned, is a two-way system. If you have ever found yourself in a one-sided conversation, you will know exactly how unpleasant it can be to have a discussion with someone who is only interested in expressing their own points of view and is not really keen or interested in what you may have to say, even though you may have some brilliant ideas. Don't just merely listen, but listen actively, give your full and undivided attention to the person who is speaking to you. Showing interest and paying attention is how you improve your communication effectiveness overall. So hone in on your listening skills as much as you do for your verbal skills. It helps.

Speaking with Clarity – Good communication means being able to be easily understood by everyone you speak to. One of the easiest ways to do that is to simply improve your speech clarity. Pronounce and enunciate your words properly, don't rush through your sentences, don't mumble, don't mutter and avoid using those conversation fillers that were talked about earlier (avoid the um's and ah's). Practice being able to put forth the messages that you want to say in as few and concise words as possible; this will help you speak with clarity because you already know exactly what needs to be said. Preparing your talking points ahead of time is another great way to boost speech clarity and keep the conversation fillers to a minimum. It also helps avoid excessive and unnecessary talking about irrelevant points, because you want your receiver to be clear about the message, not walk away from the discussion still feeling more confused about it.

Practice Friendliness – Would you enjoy speaking to someone who is unfriendly and stand-offish at the office? The obvious answer would be no. Nobody would want to engage in a conversation because they would be put off by the person's very demeanor even before they said a word. To become an effective communicator at work, you need to start adopting a friendly and approachable persona which will encourage your coworkers to want to approach you and have a conversation with you. A friendly approach is even more important when you are having a face-to-face discussion, especially if you are in a managerial position because your colleagues aren't going to want to open up to you if they feel intimidated even before the discussion has properly begun.

Be Confident – Being confident is an important part of becoming an effective communicator overall. When you interact with others around you at the workplace, the moment you show that you are confident, you will find it much easier to hold effective conversations with your colleagues and team members that will result in things getting done. Why? Because they are drawn towards your confident approach. Confident people are not thwarted by challenges, they rise to meet them, and this is what people at work want to follow: somebody who knows what they are doing and is doing it with confidence.

Say No to Distractions – Meeting rooms exist in the workplace for a reason, and it's time to make full use of them. The best way to have a meaningful conversation with the people you work with is to keep the distractions to a minimum. In an environment like work where so many people are working in close proximity with one another, phones can be constantly ringing off the hook, people will be on the move walking up and down, and several conversations could be going on at once. Not exactly the most conducive environment to hold a discussion, much less an effective conversation. Keep the distractions to a minimum, go into a meeting room and close the door, put the phones away and then when both parties are ready, begin your conversation.

Keep Your Points Consistent – To be able to deliver messages effectively means you need to be able to remain on point and consistent with what you are saying. It helps if you stick to the facts and the focus of the discussion at hand; write down and prepare your talking points before you hold the conversation. Your points should flow smoothly, and nothing should contradict each other because you could end up confusing the receiver of your message and they may become unsure about what it is you are trying to say. Your key points of your message are also at risk of being lost when you contradict yourself far too much. Plan and prepare ahead, make some notes and have them ready if you need to refer to them to help you stay on course. This is how you practice becoming a more effective communicator.

Remain as Transparent as Possible – There is nothing that is disliked more at the workplace than a lack of transparency. If you are in a leadership position especially, transparency is important in your efforts to become a more effective communicator overall. Never try to hide information, or leave out bits and pieces of information when working with your colleagues on a project or working in a team. It makes it difficult for everyone involved to communicate well if they don't have all the necessary information on hand to work with. If you are the one who is in charge of a team project, communicate clearly with your peers on what the deadlines and the goals of the project are, and ensure that everyone is clear on what needs to be done before moving forward.

No matter whether it is in your personal life or your workplace, there is no denying that communication is one of the most important skills you can develop to improve your life in all aspects. What makes it even better is that it is so easy to get started brushing up on these skills, and anyone can do it! All you need to do is just start.

Chapter 6: How to Deal with a Difficult Boss and Still Keep Your Job

Set Limits

It is important to understand your rights as a worker and to establish limits regarding your work hours and free time. Unless you have a position where you are required to be on-call, it is not reasonable or appropriate for your boss to call you during your off-hours regarding work-related matters. Let these calls go to voice mail. Listen to the messages and send a quick text to your boss saying that you are not available. You will gladly talk to them about the issue bright and early on your next scheduled workday. Furthermore, avoid being roped into staying after hours if possible. Keep in mind that once you have established the precedence of staying late or working on the weekends, this may become an expectation.

Effective Communication Skills

One of the best steps that you can take when working with a

difficult boss is to utilize effective communication skills. If your boss is the type of person who likes to provide you with half-instructions or change instructions in the middle of a project, bring a notepad with you to each meeting you have with them. Jot down any instructions they provide. Before you leave their presence, repeat the instructions that you have written down. This will accomplish two things. First, it provides your boss with the ability to add to the instructions before you begin working on the project. Second, it makes you look as though you are diligent and committed to following through on their instructions perfectly. It may be wise to follow up with your boss about the status of a project several times to ensure that your work meets their expectations.

Maintain Distance

It is important to maintain distance from your boss as much as possible. This is a person who you must work with and must take instructions from, but this does not mean that you need to hang out with the person all of the time. You can decrease your annoyance with this person and keep your blood pressure lower by working on your own as much as possible. Also, avoid extra-curricular activities with your boss outside of the office. If you are permitted to, consider working from home as much as possible. Do what you need to do to keep your job and not appear to be standoffish. However, the distance can be healthy when dealing with someone who irritates you.

Many people will deal with a difficult boss at one point or another. How you manage your relationship with this person will ultimately affect your sanity and your ability to keep your job. Following these strategies will help you more effectively when dealing with your difficult boss.

Chapter 7: Choosing to Get Better at Explaining Things at Work

I believe its common knowledge that the workplace is one of diversity and differing opinions on any subject matter. You will rarely find two people who agree without striving to have the upper hand or a monopoly on being correct. Some workers really underestimate or simply don't care about the importance of workplace communication. Communication is either effective or ineffective. When workplace communication is chaotic, it could affect the quality of your customer service and impact your customer base by driving them to your competitor.

Managers play a key role in understanding the information relayed to them by the people they manage. When the wrong information is given, the manager will make bad decisions based on such information. Employees have an equally important role and responsibility in making sure that a matter is properly and accurately explained. This is essential for obvious reasons. For instance, when an employee places a trouble call to IT stating that his or her computer is broken, this tells the IT department nothing. When technicians use proper troubleshooting techniques (asking questions) to find out what the real issue is, the valuable tie was squandered on a process because one person did not want to take the time to explain the problem with the correct details.

This is only one of the many examples. Employees and coworkers alike who work in one company should have one major goal, and that is staying employed; to do that requires that you do the job you are paid for. Yes, explaining things does take time and attention. Maybe for some, it's an acquired skill, however it is a significant part of your interaction in the workplace. In a down economy, one person could very well be the cause of losing valuable customers because of one's inability to explain a matter. This is why managers must train, inspire and convey to those whom they manage the importance of stating the facts properly and accurately.

Employees must choose to get better at explaining. Why? One day you may be replaced by someone who is better at it. If you are a business owner, it will simply cost you money. If you are a leader of an organization, it will cost you in resources. Either way, the inability to give a proper and correct explanation that can be easily understood will cost the giver and the receiver. We live in an age where information is powerful thus bad or misunderstood information can be harmful and even dangerous. When it comes to communicating, you are either the sender or the receiver of the information; often you are doing both. It's the personal responsibility of the one explaining, who often finds one's ability to convey is lacking, and thus it is essential to take necessary steps to improve.

Chapter 8: Communicating Up, Across and Out

Nearly all of us have a complicated set of relationships to manage and navigate at the office. The relationships that require the most work are those that involve communicating upwards; that is, directly or indirectly to bosses and senior influencers.

Communicating with Bosses

There are limitations on how much "strength" you can bring to these communications, and unfortunately it varies from boss to boss. Projecting too much "strength" to an insecure boss may be interpreted as a threat. On the other extreme, a very aggressive boss may want a show of "strength" from you when you are making a case for a new project or budget proposal. One of the tried and tested techniques for projecting "warmth" with just about any personality type is to appeal to concerns that will help your boss either look good or avoid trouble.

If, for instance, you are able to pass along useful intelligence because you have an ally in another office higher up the food chain, your boss can prepare for incoming fire before it reaches his/her desk through formal channels.

The "no surprises" rule is another that's tried and true; most bosses appreciate advance warning about developments or issues that may end up on their desks. This projects "warmth" by demonstrating your loyalty to the team.

If your boss is one who gives you a relatively free rein, proactive engagement can be a good way of shaping your own agenda and demonstrating your competence as a self-starter. With micromanagers however, many respond well to a steady flow of information about your activities. Micromanagers are typically high in two aspects of "strength": competence and assertiveness. Regular reminders that you also value competence can be a good way to set your micromanager's mind at ease. Whether your organization talks in terms of shareholder value, key performance indicators, project milestones, or team goals and objectives, the micromanager will appreciate hearing that you share their passion in hitting those same targets.

With Subordinates

When communicating with people at lower levels in the organization, it is important to keep in mind that they may see you differently than you see yourself. If you are an unknown quantity, it can be important to establish a basis for respect. This can be achieved through a combination of the words you choose and nonverbal cues, including posture and dressing.

In other cases, your position may confer status that gives you a halo, or it may make you a source of resentment. This is particularly common in organizations where there is a clear line between management, and "the field." One potential way to protect yourself against this is to acknowledge it in a lighthearted way at the outset. By demonstrating that you are aware of how they feel about you, you can disarm skeptics and help establish "warmth" that can serve as a basis for building a solid working relationship.

Chapter 9: Importance of Effective Communication in the Workplace

Promotes a Healthy Work Environment

One of the most important aspects of a successful organization is employee motivation. People are more likely to perform their duties well when effective communication is established between employees and management because everyone knows what is expected of them. Frustration and confusion in the workplace is reduced when the lines of communication between these two parties are open.

Helps Remove Cultural Barriers

Without effective communication, workplace diversity can cause a lot of misunderstandings. Language and cultural differences can be managed when everyone is able to understand and practice proper communication in the workplace.

Lessens Absenteeism and Turnover Rate

Effective communication in the workplace is a good predictor of job satisfaction because employees who understand their roles and are able to have both upward and downward communication tend to be more satisfied with their jobs. Good communication in the workplace allows for the healthy flow of ideas, opinions and concerns which can have positive effects on absenteeism and turnover rates.

Fosters Teamwork and Professional Relationships

Teamwork and professional relationships are strengthened when effective communication is practiced because difficult or negative messages can be properly communicated without damaging trust or creating conflict.

Effective Communication Forms and Maintains Relationships and Rapport

At the workplace, it is important to maintain positive and amicable relationships with your coworkers. You are going to spend most your day working together with them, and without the proper communication skills on hand, it can be difficult to build and construct productive relationships with the ones you work with.

Effective Communication Promotes Innovation

Innovation at the workplace increases when its employees are comfortable and confident enough to openly communicate their ideas and work well with one another. When employees are not able to communicate their exact thoughts and ideas, or if they don't feel confident enough to do so, the chances of good ideas ever being implemented in the workplace become slim to none.

Effective Communication Builds Better Teamwork

When effective communication flows freely in the workplace, it is easier to build teams which are productive and cohesive, who work well together to get things done. When employees within a team can communicate and get along well with one another, the staff morale is given a boost because they feel confident in what they are doing. When the management communicates the company's mission and vision effectively, the employees will in turn feel more secure in their roles and be able to perform better as a result. Work ethics are also improved when internal communication within a company is excellent because the staff fully understand what common goal it is that they are working towards. Effective Communication Can Boost the Growth of the Company – A company relies on effective marketing to generate business and sales. Marketing is about delivering strong messages across to the clients, making sure that those messages hit the target right where they are supposed to. How is this done? By relying on effective communication. Communication, especially in the marketing role, is crucial because, without the great marketing collateral, good communication internally and externally becomes a struggle for the company. When the company starts to struggle, it is only a matter of time before it folds because it is not able to work to overcome those barriers.

Effective Communication Helps Promote Transparency

Transparency at the workplace is important to help build trust in the brand. This trust must be gained both internally among the employees, and externally among the clients. Trust is one of the fundamental reasons clients will keep coming back to you, and why employees remain loyal to your company. Transparency and effective communication go hand-in-hand because when it comes time for tough decisions to be made, the company leaders will have a much easier time explaining why to their employees if they practice effective communication.

Effective Communication Helps Workplace Diversity

Today's workplace is a melting pot of diverse cultures and

languages. For everyone to be able to mesh well together and work in harmony, it is important to have good communication skills handy. Being able to communicate well will help to reduce the cultural and language barriers, and companies who know this will understand the importance of providing communication training for both their local and international employees. Effective communication will avoid confusion and misunderstanding, allowing company operations to run much smoother when everyone can work well together.

Effective Communication Will Boost Customer Service

If you are going to provide top-notch service to your clients, you are going to need to be able to understand what they want. Exactly what they want. If you don't, there is no way you are going to be able to meet their needs or even go the extra mile to deliver the best service you possibly can. No matter what you may be selling, your relationship with your clients relies heavily on your ability to be able to communicate effectively, because you need to be able to convince them why they should go along with your business instead of your competitors.

Chapter 10: Communication Skills in the Workplace

Verbal Communication Skills

Open Door Policy

To create a culture of effective communication in the workplace, managers must be as transparent and as straightforward as possible. Doing so fosters trust and understanding within an organization.

Employees must know that they can approach their manager at any time. To create this sense, managers can enforce an open door policy for all employees, regardless of the employee's position. Below are some suggestions for an effective open door policy:

Listen with Your Full Attention

As a manager, you must be able to accommodate and attend to the concerns of your employees. It's your job to make them feel heard and to show that you are willing to lend a helping hand.

Re-schedule and Follow-through

If you are in the middle of something, re-schedule politely and ask your employee to come back at another time. Just make sure that you get back to him or her when you are no longer busy.

Establish a Limit

When an employee abuses his right to come to your office, ask the human resources department to mediate. Or if possible, address the issue by yourself first. Explain the nature of the employee's transgression and make suggestions for improvement.

Be Clear in Assigning Tasks

Employees are more productive when they know exactly what is expected of them. When assigning tasks, make sure that you are clear and direct.

Avoid using terms that may confuse the person who you are trying to communicate with and replace inflated words with simpler terms to make everything more understandable.

Think Before You Speak

Emotions can interfere with our thoughts and actions but as a manager, it is crucial that you think before speaking and always appear calm. To improve your communication skills, consider all the facts and review the entire situation before making any kind of decision or taking action.

Be Open to Criticism

As a manager, it is important that you approach all problems in a professional manner. If your management skills are criticized, consider the validity of the critiques and try to improve.

Make Sure That You are Understood

A good manager makes sure that he or she is clear and understood by his or her employees. As a manager, you must oversee your team's process, but you must also ensure that your employees understand their tasks completely.

To make sure that you're understood, try to manage individuals instead of groups. Groups lack specificity which may reduce individual feelings of accountability and create a free-rider problem in the office. Use memos that address the majority when you are trying to disseminate general information, but when it comes to giving out directions or individual criticisms, it is best if they are done face-to-face or in private.

Nonverbal Communication Skills

Nonverbal cues are fairly easy to overlook, but they are crucial to interpersonal communication. Unintended nonverbal signals may send confusing messages or lead to misunderstandings when not managed effectively.

Eye Contact and Facial Expression

Maintaining eye contact and a pleasant expression usually signals that you are open to communication. Regardless of your mood, maintain eye contact and be aware of your facial expression. If you want to be a better communicator, you have to be mindful of these nonverbal cues.

Body Language

Nonverbal signals can say a lot. Be conscious of how you stand, sit, walk, and hold your head. Subtle movements, posture, and stance can send out a lot of wrong signals to others: your words may say one thing while your body is saying another. It is important to be mindful of these nonverbal cues in the workplace to avoid misinterpretation.

Written Communication Skills

Managers must also be equipped with good, written communication skills to fulfill their duties properly. The quality of a professional manager's writing will have a huge impact on his or her career and organization because the exchange of information within and outside any organization is done through writing. To help you improve your writing skills, here are some basic tips:

Know Your Objectives

Before putting your thoughts into writing, you have to define your goals. Establishing a specific objective will help you be concise and straightforward when trying to get your message across. In defining your goals, it is also important to consider your audience: be mindful of what they already know, what they need to know, and what you want to tell them.

Style and Structure

In writing business or corporate documents, you don't have to use fancy language or hard to understand metaphors. The goal of writing in the workplace should be to send and disseminate information so the structure should be focused on making the document clear and organized. For example, try starting paragraphs with the main topic, and then follow the main topic up with further explanation or analogy.

Draft, Review, Edit

Now that you have established your objectives, identified your audience and written your message in an organized fashion, the next step is to re-read, edit and make sure that all of your points were explained well.

Chapter 11: Steps for Developing Effective Workplace Communication Skills

Communication has three main styles – verbal, nonverbal and written. All of these are needed in running a business. Some employees may be good in verbal communication, but have problems effectively communicating through emails and letters. Others can be excellent in verbal and written communication, but may have trouble ensuring that their body language matches their words. Companies need to train their employees so that they can master all three styles of communication. Fortunately, barriers in communication can be eliminated and, with time and practice, all people can communicate effectively. Here are some useful tips on how to improve one's communication skills:

Step 1

Always use words that are easy to understand. If you had to

choose between using a difficult vocabulary and an easy one, always choose the easy word. That way, you are sure that your listener will understand. Relaying important messages is not the time to impress people with your high knowledge of vocabulary. Remember that your goal is to deliver to your coworkers important information and that you should help them understand it. Don't confuse your target audience by making your words and sentences more complex than they should be. In fact, you should be simplifying your message to reduce any chances of misinterpretation. Speak clearly and use concise sentences to deliver your message.

Step 2

Many people who are great public speakers have some difficulty when it comes to written communication. Writing is very different from speaking, and written communication is a skill that should also be mastered. It is quite necessary in business communication. Some CEO's even have staff members write letters and messages for them. So if you are given the task of communicating with your boss, colleague, subordinate or workmates, never take it for granted. Write a draft and, just like in verbal communication, always choose clear, concise words to deliver your message. You actually have an advantage in written communication because, unlike verbal communication, you can check for errors and edit your message until you are satisfied.

Step 3

Managers and supervisors should learn how to practice open body language when delivering messages to their subordinates. This is done by taking a non-aggressive stance, such as putting both arms at the side of the body, avoiding abrupt gestures and adapting a relaxed posture and a friendly facial expression. Open body language works well for all employees. It creates a non-threatening atmosphere when communicating. Also, always face the person you are talking to and make sure that you have good eye contact.

Step 4

Perfect the art of listening. Many individuals have no trouble winning the hearts and minds of people around them by just showing their ability to really listen. Communicating is not only about speaking and delivering your message. It is also about receiving what the other party has to share. That way, there is two-way communication and the conversation is made whole. There are times when employees need to talk about their concerns and voice their issues. Workers, managers and bosses need to practice listening to each other in order to help the company run smoothly. Problems arise when one fails to listen to the other.

Step 5

Attend lectures and take courses to better your communication skills. Who says you've learned all that you need to know? People and situations change every day and we should learn to adapt to all of these changes. There are always new ways and methods to communicate more effectively. Keep abreast of the changes and developments, and learn as much as you can about being able to communicate more effectively.

Chapter 12: Common Communication Mistakes to Avoid

No one is immune to communication mistakes, but as often as possible, we should try to avoid making these mistakes. Effective communication in the workplace requires employees to carefully consider the needs of their audience, to mindfully prepare presentations (e.g. reports, memos, emails, and other documents), and to ready themselves for follow-up questions.

Misunderstandings and conflict in the workplace can be reduced if everyone makes an effort to avoid some of the most common communication mistakes. To help you understand these mistakes better, here are some of the most common communication mistakes that you should be mindful of:

Failing to Review and Double-Check Everything

Mistakenly sending a client the wrong price list or sending confidential data to your coworkers can cost you your job. All emails and documents should be handled with the utmost care so as to avoid accidentally violating a person or your company's privacy. Carefully edit sensitive messages and always double-check that that the recipients, message, and attachments in an email are all correct.

Additionally, a lack of preparation before sharing a presentation or report can quickly affect your credibility. Before delivering a speech, rehearse and prepare it so that errors can be spotted and prevented.

Being Insensitive to Cultural Differences

If you work in a culturally diverse organization, keeping an open mind is a must. It is important to not let stereotypes affect your judgment because making general assumptions about people based on their background, culture or preferences can hinder effective and open communication in the workplace.

Generalizing

Another common communication mistake is assuming that everyone embraces a single or universal approach to learning. Generalizing means overlooking the fact that people digest information in different ways. A communicator must address these differences and consider an approach that caters to people with different learning styles.

Not Being Able to Say No

Have you ever been asked to lead a project or take on additional responsibility when your plate is already full? Overwhelming yourself isn't helpful, and if you're spread too thin, then your performance is compromised. If you have a valid excuse, it's okay to turn down a task. Being assertive means having the ability to state your needs while keeping in mind the requests and needs of others.

Avoiding Difficult Conversations

When you see a colleague or superior make a mistake, don't hesitate to point it out. Avoiding difficult conversations doesn't solve problems and might even make them worse. At some point in your life, you will have to deliver negative feedback. As an effective communicator, you must be able to handle difficult conversations with clarity and accuracy, and one step in this direction is to face difficult conversations head on.

Similarly, you must keep in mind that it is unethical to send bad news through an email, text, or a third party. Deliver sensitive messages in person, and try your best to stay calm.

Letting Emotions Take Over

Being professional in the workplace is crucial which is why you have to learn to properly manage your emotions at work. Effective communication cannot take place when your emotions are in the way, and flying off the handle is never permissible. Try your best to handle issues and manage conflict with calmness and objectivity.

Not Following Up with Your Audience

Assuming that everyone immediately absorbs your message is impractical. Confirm that your message was received and understood by asking your audience if they have any questions or need anything explained further. During oral presentations, ask your audience to summarize your main points to make sure that your message was clear.

Female Body Language Mistakes

For all you ladies out there, here's a list of body language mistakes you need to avoid, especially if you want to be taken seriously at work, or even otherwise:

Acting girlish.

Girlish behavior consists of, and are not limited to, twirling your hair, playing with jewelry, biting your nails, fidgeting with your clothes, hugging your own body, etc. I understand you can do all this almost involuntarily, but try to keep a check on it, especially if you're in an authoritative position in your office. Doing this can decrease the sense of power and authority others usually associate with you.

Nodding too much.

Stick to the rule of nodding once every three sentences completed by the person you're interacting with. Nods express you're paying attention; it encourages the other person to continue speaking. But too many nods don't speak authority and power. It feels like you're too eager to please the other person - you're not the boss. So, claim your authority and power by limiting your nods.

Learn to interrupt.

When you're the boss or an important member of your organization, don't wait for your turn to be allowed to speak. When you've got something to say, just say it, or else others will just run you over. Speak out to say your piece to maintain your authority and power, especially in meetings, negotiations, etc.

Don't be too expressive.

To increase the sense of authority and power people usually associate with you at your workplace, try to put a rein on your movements. By this I mean you need to firm or control your emotions at work. This means no mood swings, bouts of nervousness, etc. To look powerful, put on a calm and contained front.

These are the four common mistakes you should avoid at your workplace. And of course, you can keep these in mind even outside your workplace.

You don't need to be pushy to create a niche of your own inside or outside your workplace, but you have to express yourself properly to be taken seriously by everyone and anyone. And to accomplish this, you have to pay attention to your body language, in addition to your verbal and written communication skills.

If you're "leaking" bad communication through your body language, it's time to put a stop to it immediately.

Chapter 13: Techniques to Develop and Display Open-mindedness, Empathy and Respect in Workplace Communication

Many people reach a certain level of success in their careers due to excellent technical abilities or other attractive hard skills like earning a certificate or degree, but because their people skills are lacking, it hampers their effectiveness because they don't get along well with other team members. Employees with poor people skills often find themselves at the center of unnecessary conflict which results in a stressful situation for everyone involved with negative consequences that can sidetrack the best-laid project plans.

When it comes to attaining hard skills, people are usually confident they can develop new skills through education, training, and experience. But when it comes to "soft" skills that deal with interacting with other people, they aren't so sure. People who say they aren't "a people person" often don't believe you can gain new skills to help in those areas because they embrace the idea that you just are what you are and there's nothing you can do about it, but that is not the case. For those who want to improve their soft skills, empathy is a great place to start to improve your people skills.

So where do you start? It boils down to communication again. You start by improving your verbal communication and related interpersonal skills. What does one have to do with the other? To be empathic, you need to be able to think beyond yourself and your concerns and to develop the ability to empathize with others. This takes communication, and as a bonus, once you start to understand others, they will start to understand you.

Techniques to Help Develop Empathy

Put aside your own point of view: Work toward seeing things from the other person's viewpoint. As you start to do this more and more, it will become clearer that other people aren't being unreasonable, unkind or stubborn, but are most likely reacting to the information they have.

Acknowledge the other person's perspective: Once you come to see what the other person thinks and why they believe what they do, acknowledge their perspective. People do have differences of opinion, and reasons to support their views. Acknowledgement of this doesn't mean you agree with them but it is a step toward being better able to work together.

Take a closer look at your attitude: A winning attitude does not mean getting your own way, being right, or even winning. If this is your attitude, then you don't have an open mind or an empathetic attitude. In fact, such an attitude shows you most likely won't have room for empathy in your life unless you change. Work toward a new priority – a change in thinking regarding what's important. Focus on things like finding a solution, building relationships and accepting others and it will help you change from the inside out.

Become a better listener: Do you notice how this skill pops up repeatedly? Learning to listen is often more important than learning what to say. To become more empathetic, learn to listen to the complete message the other person is sending while using active listening techniques. Be sure to practice "listening" with your heart to hear what the other person is feeling too. When you're unclear about what they are saying, ask them to explain their position, and don't be afraid to ask them what they want. This not only shows you're listening but that you are interested and actually care.

Putting these skills into practice will give you the appearance of being more caring and approachable as you interact with people because you are showing an interest in what other people think, feel, and experience. As you work on developing empathy, you can use this short checklist as a reminder of what to do, as you practice interacting with others through conversation:

Notice physically and mentally what's happening.

Give them your full attention and listen carefully to what they are saying. Note the key words and phrases used.

Respond receptively to the main theme of their message.

Developing Open-Mindedness

One of the reasons many people have poor people skills is because the isolate themselves from interaction. This tends to create close-mindedness as people become set on their own viewpoint. Improving verbal communication skills can change this because communication allows you to connect with others and build relationships and through them change your thinking, earn respect, acquire influence, and become more likable. Practice the following techniques to grow these skills and develop a more open mind:

Be approachable: Communicate using a friendly tone and warm smile. This approach draws people to you because subconsciously it makes them feel good.

Think before you speak: Often people think being blunt and speaking whatever is on their mind is a good thing. The problem is it ends up reflecting poorly on them. Learn to think before you speak because if you're not careful with your words, you can destroy the very thing you're trying to build.

Be clear: In today's world of tight schedules, people don't have the time or energy to figure out what someone is "trying" to say. Avoid being indirect or hinting at the point you are trying to make without saying what you really mean. Challenge yourself to speak directly making your message clear.

Avoid talking too much: People tend to listen to those who carefully choose their words. On the other hand, people often lose their audience if they talk too much, and those who talk more than they should also run the risk of sharing information unnecessarily.

Be authentic: You don't have to pretend to be something you're not or put on a show to get people to listen to what you have to say. In fact, people are attracted to those who are transparent and speak from the heart.

How to Demonstrate Respect in the Workplace

Learning to demonstrate respect helps to avoid needless, insensitive, unmeant disrespect. Showing respect can be done in small ways that are simple and yet powerful in the way people perceive you. The following list is straightforward, and truthfully you probably won't find things you don't know, but you probably will find some that you don't put into practice. Make it your goal to show and encourage more respect in your workplace:

Treat coworkers with courtesy, politeness, and kindness.

Encourage others to voice their opinions and ideas.

Before you express your point of view, listen to what others have to say.

Don't speak over, interrupt, or cut off another person when they are speaking.

Use other people's ideas to make changes or improve things at work. Be sure to let them know you used their idea or encourage them to implement the idea themselves.

Avoid insulting anyone. No name calling, no putting down people or their ideas.

Don't be a nitpicker. Constantly criticizing, belittling, or patronizing might seem trivial at the time, but it adds up and actually is a form of bullying. Needless to say, it doesn't cultivate respect.

Make a conscious effort to improve your ability to interact with those around you at work. This means both bosses and coworkers. This will show them that you've grown more aware of the people around you and will open the opportunity to be more sympathetic.

Be sure to treat everyone the same and implement policies and procedures in a consistent manner so people feel they are being treated both equally and fairly.

Praise people much more often than you criticize. Also encourage employees to praise and recognize each other's accomplishments.

These ideas can help you lay a good foundation of respect. Once you consciously work at showing respect, you may be surprised to learn it is actually a cornerstone of meaningful work. Practicing respect won't just change you but will actually affect those around you too as the environment around you develops into a respectful, considerate, professional workplace. Improving your verbal and nonverbal communication skills requires intentional effort and an increased awareness and desire to improve. Your efforts to develop and display open-mindedness, empathy and respect in the ways you communicate will enhance your relationships, increase your self-esteem, and increase your value in the workplace.

Chapter 14: How to be Proactive in Workplace Communication

Effective communication requires both an internal and external management emphasis. Managers must be receptive, using effective inquiry to enhance the quality of interaction with their employees. This raises levels of awareness and understanding among both parties, resulting in more effective solutions to existing issues and problems. Effective communication encompasses two basic approaches:

The Receiving and Interpreting Approach

Managers need to be aware that communication alone doesn't sufficiently influence employees to become collectively involved in the resolution of major issues or concerns. To do this, a leader's communication must be proactive. When volatile issues and problems surface, proactive communication becomes the only effective weapon to defuse them. For managers to communicate proactively, they must be able to receive and interpret the right messages and respond in a way that leads to resolution. This means managers must pay particular attention to applying the receiving and interpreting approach that focuses upon:

Eliminating "half-baked" listening. Often managers can be off-focus in their listening habits. They can lean forward, nodding to affirm they are hearing what's being said and can even repeat back word-for-word what was stated, but they may not be listening at all.

Desiring to form personal opinions about what employees are saying, they short-circuit their listening efforts. They often begin formulating the next step in their argument or message to convince or influence an individual to agree with their opinions or suggestions. This approach removes the proactive structure from communication. When this occurs, managers do not listen at all, but simply act as though they do.

Managers need to continually apply the internal proactive practice of setting aside judgments, assumptions, reactions and inaccurate interpretations. Doing so creates space for genuinely receiving employees' contributions to the conversation. This technique allows managers to gather critical information that often changes their perspectives or increases their understanding of specific issues and points that are necessary to refer to.

The Inquiry Approach

The inquiry is a key element of dialogue. Applying inquiring phrases is another way managers can move beyond preconceptions of what their people are or should be saying, or how they should perceive things.

Two specific types of inquiries proactively work to aid effective communication between managers and employees. These are:

"Why do you say that?"

This inquiry is effective for defusing volatile situations and gaining the accurate intention and interpretation behind hurtful, divisive, aggressive or hostile comments. It is also effective to use when participants become defensive or reactionary. This type of inquiry breaks the negative pattern of the conversation, allowing for a more beneficial exchange of ideas, comments or suggestions.

"What are your thoughts on the matter?"

This inquiry style is a twofold proactive communication application. It clarifies the statement or perspective shared by an individual and also works effectively to change the complexion of a heated conversation. It settles people down and diminishes negative or reactionary verbal comments while creating personal accountability for their statements and responses.

Overcoming Barriers to Proactive Communication

Managers must have an arsenal of proactive techniques at their disposal to help them communicate effectively and resolve employee-related issues and problems before they get out of control.

There are several techniques managers can effectively use to create an open and meaningful dialogue between themselves and their employees to solve problems, issues, and concerns. In all conversations and dialogues managers need to:

Set the stage with background information regarding an existing issue or problem while offering some general advice and guidelines for discussion.

Select a proper setting for the conversation or discussion, including whether it is better to have a group discussion or a one-to-one encounter.

Make certain to have the employee's undivided attention before initiating a conversation or discussion. Sit close to and directly face them.

Demonstrate continuous interest by maintaining direct eye contact while leaning forward. Always be conscious of facial expressions and other body language.

Apply multiple forms of nonverbal communication, such as gesturing, pointing, writing and drawing.

Speak forcefully but clearly. Don't exaggerate words, phrases or meanings.

Maintain a lower pitch in voice quality. A low-pitched tone generates more of a desire for continued listening than a strained or higher tone.

Be patient, remain calm, and allow others the time they need to communicate their message. Resist the urge to interrupt or finish sentences to move the communication process along, unless the individual gets frustrated to the point where it is obvious he or she needs help completing a thought. When this happens, managers should ask if they are interpreting and responding correctly to the actual intention of the individual's thought.

Be attuned to nonverbal language offering clues to the factual or emotional content of the employee's message.

Consistently summarize the individual's message to ensure it has been heard correctly.

Refrain from correcting grammar and language errors.

Continually ask sincere, relevant questions before advocating points or thoughts regarding an issue or concern.

Respond to comments and messages—never react.

Offer specific and positive feedback whenever appropriate.

Keep responses brief. This affords employees the best opportunity to understand and remember the main points of the message.

Chapter 15: Working with Poor Communicators

Many of you may have been reminded of coworkers while reading through this book. Unfortunately, we all know people who are not effective communicators. Of all the communications you will have during your working life, none of them will stick with you as vividly as the ones that failed miserably to accurately share the necessary information.

Communication is a two-way street. So, when you are communicating with these poor communicators, whether as a sender or recipient, there are things you can do to help them. This does not mean telling them they are doing things wrong or suggesting they read this book. Part of what you should be doing to become a better communicator is learning the communication styles and needs of the people you communicate with.

Know Who You Are Talking To

Whenever you are communicating, you need to know who is on the other side of the conversation. You need to learn which styles and tones they use and which they are most likely to receive without complications. Some people are better on the phone. Others do not understand the forms they are supposed to be in charge of. Knowing these things allows you to adjust your communications whether you are initiating or responding.

This may not be something you can do rapidly. That is okay. Communication is an ongoing learning process. Do not think that every communication will be successful. Just focus on preparing, participating, and reviewing your conversations for both the good and bad from all participants. If someone in your office has been having a really hard time getting back to emails, then adjust your communications to allow for that.

Follow Up

You should always follow up on your conversations. Some people, however, will require more follow up than others. You may be able to get away with a short email to some coworkers and feel confident that the information has been adequately conveyed. If you find that there are always failures in your communications with certain individuals, then you need to increase your follow up with them. Send them an email and then call to discuss it with them to clear up any confusion or misunderstanding. If you run into them in the hallway and they tell you about a new project, then send them an email about it when you get back to your desk.

Sometimes responses will not be immediate. Place a calendar reminder for yourself to follow up. One of the biggest hurdles for communication is time. In the modern business world we do not have the luxury of focusing on one conversation from start to finish. We are so connected to everything that we often find ourselves distracted by a number of conversations at any given time. It is entirely possible that anyone at any time will forget about any singular conversation they are involved in.

Get Confirmation

It would be a great world if we could just trust that everything everyone said was true. This is not the reality we live in. If someone says something that does not seem correct, then get confirmation on it. This may mean repeating it back to them or it may mean getting confirmation from another department.

Some people have a tendency to very confidently state assumptions and opinions in a way that portrays them as facts. These individuals will most likely never stop communicating with their undue sense of confidence or importance. Therefore, you must be vigilant in how you communicate with them. Avoid confronting them directly if you can, but if it becomes a consistent problem, you may need to have a conversation with them or their superiors about how they communicate.

Keep Records

Always save questionable emails or anything that needs clarification. If it was a phone call, then document it afterwards. Important meetings should always have someone taking minutes, but if you need to write something up afterwards, that is okay too. One of the hardest things about confronting a poor communicator is that they will have a hard time communicating about the problem. Having records of the conversations will make it easier to show them what was said and how it was understood.

You should also document the impact of any failed communications. If scheduling failed to communicate a deadline, then make a record of the costs of expedited shipping or lost sales. Make sure you capture the real, bottom line impacts of what happened. You do not want to just be someone complaining about how another person in your workplace communicates, because that will only make people more defensive or outright hostile in how they communicate with you.

Be Patient

Not everyone is an effective communicator. Just remember that you are someone who cared enough to read this book. Most of your coworkers will not. Go into each day prepared to patiently engage your coworkers in the most effective communication you can help create. Take pride when you help share information effectively within your organization and forgive the poor communicators for their shortcomings. Life is too short to get upset over a poorly crafted email or cryptic phone call.

Chapter 16: Critical Communications in the Workplace

When we get older and enter into the workplace, we are going to be thrust into a world of totally different experiences that will change on a daily basis. When this occurs, it is vital that we have a wide range of communications skills that will allow us to manipulate our world, the businesses that we work for and with these communications achieve our ultimate goals.

Mindset on our jobs

When we start a new job, we are filled with excitement, fear and anticipation. We are entering into a new environment of uncertainty that we need to learn from and develop an understanding from. This is where our mindset takes top priority.

Depending on the type of job you have and the tasks that you are asked to perform, it may be difficult to have a positive and outgoing mindset. For example, if you have a job that doesn't pay a lot of money, has long hours and a lot of physical labor, then you may feel mentally and physically unhealthy. When this occurs, your mindset may be just to go in and do what you have to do and get your check.

Unfortunately, this is not the kind of mindset that you should have. When entering into any job, you need to have a positive mindset and take every action that you have as one step closer to your ultimate goal.

When you start out having a positive mindset, you will be more focused physically and emotionally and as such communicate better and achieve more success.

Mindset towards employees and management

When it comes to your mindset towards other employees and upper management, the more positive your mindset, the easier it will be to communicate with them. The first thing that you need to understand is that those who come to work with you are in the same situation as you. They need to come to the place of employment, perform tasks that they may or may not like to do and have to deal with the stress of customers right alongside you.

When you can do this, communication becomes much easier. This is first done by education. Since you are all in the same place of employment, you can learn how others perform their tasks. You can see where their strengths are, where their weaknesses lie and how you can best communicate with them to get the desired results you are looking for.

Working and communicating at work

When you have developed your mindset, you need to start developing your communication skills and protocol. Since you are in a working environment, there will be a lot more ways to communicate with others than in a standard everyday environment.

What happens at work stays at work

The first thing that you need to realize is that you are in a work environment where you are dealing with customers, customer data and a lot of confidential information. With this in mind, it is vital that whatever happens at work stays at work. This means that you can't talk about clients or customers outside of work. You can't talk about company policies, actions of other employees or content along these lines. If you do, you could be putting the health and well-being of the company at risk as well as opening yourself up for a lawsuit or even getting fired. So when communicating at work, make sure to keep all communications internal.

Have open meetings

When communicating at work, it is vital that people know what is going on. With open meetings everyone in the company should understand and feel free to voice their opinions. In these meetings there may come occasions where certain individuals need to be singled out for one reason or another. To help keep the health and morality of employees and the overall opinion of the business intact, certain sensitive information or personal conflict conversations should be kept private.

In these meetings the focus should be on the overall growth and expansion of the business, not a witch hunt for problems or blame parties. Make your meetings a safe environment for everyone and your business will be better for it.

Emails

Emails are a great way to communicate with employees, management and even customers. With this being said, sending emails need to be well protected and content and information should be setup securely so that information doesn't fall into the wrong hands.

For example, there should be a dedicated email address setup that is only used for sending out messages to customers. This email address should be setup on a dedicated computer or under a specific account that needs to be specifically logged into. If sensitive information or even a hate email were to accidently get out to your customer database, it could mean the end of the business.

When sending emails to others in the office, these emails should only be about company business and must not contain personal information or about non-work related topics. In simpler terms, don't send an email to Jim talking about Sarah. Keep that type of communications off work systems.

One-on-one communications

When in the office, interoffice chatter is going to be a given. People will be walking by your desk asking questions, delivering supplies, asking for updates on projects and more. When it comes time to talk to a specific employee about a personal topic or of a sensitive nature, it is important that these one-on-one conversations be handled in private. You should never have a one-on-one conversation in a group. This will look bad to everyone. Also, if you need to fire an employee or reprimand him or her, do it before work or at the end of the day when others are not in the office.

Be clear and concise in your requests

When working in a business, it is vital that people understand what it is that you are looking for. If you are assigning an employee a project or a specific task, make sure that everything is laid out for them in a step by step fashion. If they have questions, make sure that you are available to them to answer these questions and don't get angry or upset if they come to you multiple times with the same question. If they do, then make sure to answer it professionally. If at the end of the task they didn't complete it to your satisfaction, then you can take appropriate actions.

Make it a safe environment

When it comes to working in an office or any place of business, it needs to be a safe environment. If people find a problem, they need to know that it is safe to come to you in order to solve it. If an issue needs to be fixed, it needs to be fixed as soon as possible and people don't need to feel that their words are going unheard.

Use the appropriate voice and tone of voice

When communicating with others it isn't always what you say but how you say it. When people feel that your tone is angry, loud and unsettling, they will take it as a personal reflection on their actions. This is why you need to understand body language, voice inflections and other traits of people. When you can read what is being said without words, you can better handle the situation without being offended or angry.

Have a sense of humor

No one wants a wet blanket or someone they need to walk on eggshells for. This is where mindset comes in again. If you are someone who doesn't like his or her job or the people who you are working with, then you need to find another job. If it is an environment that you don't really want to be in, then you need to use your communication skills to help transform it into this type of environment. When you inject humor into different situations you are communicating in, it is a fun and enjoyable environment. Just make sure that you are not making fun of or poking fun at others who might take it the wrong way.

Articulate

When communicating with others, you want to articulate your meanings. Don't just assume that others will know and understand what it is you are trying to convey. Make sure that you use additional mediums such as charts, graphs, videos, and audio to get your point across. When you can do this effectively, you have raised your communication game to the next level.

Encourage feedback

One of the best ways to allow a company to grow is to encourage feedback. When you allow others to give their feedback and voice their opinions, you get a wealth of ideas and options that you can then discuss and grow from. If you don't encourage feedback, you could be missing the boat as it were and as such doing more harm than good.

Be appreciative

Showing your appreciation to others will help strengthen and grow the lines of communication at the workplace. When people feel that their words are welcomed and even encouraged, it goes a long way and helps create a safe environment. If, on the other hand, you reject all of your employees' ideas and don't show any appreciation for their hard work and dedication, it will quickly become reflective in their performance and overall mental health towards their job.

Encourage team building

Another great way to encourage communication and creativity is through team building. When you build teams of people, they learn to better communicate with themselves as well as others. When you have strong teams working together, your company will become very productive and hopefully profitable.

At the end of the day we all have to work. Making the work environment fun and open for communications will go a long way towards your bottom line.

Chapter 17: Top Tips and Tricks for Workplace Communication

At this point, I would like to give you some tips and tricks that you can implement into your communication skills. When it comes to communication, it is a skill just like reading, writing and math. The more you practice and the more skills you acquire, the better off you will be when you actually find yourself in specific situations.

Body Language

When it comes to communication, your body language plays a key role in how you and your world are perceived. The first thing that you need to master is eye contact. When we talk to people, if we can get them to look into our eyes, we can begin to tell if they are lying, hiding something or are nervous. Eye contact is a key component in all communication.

Keep your head raised up high. Another component in body language is how we hold up our heads. When we raise our heads up high and can look eye to eye with others, it shows a level of confidence. When we have our heads hanging down low or we are moving our heads around looking at other things in the room, it is a telltale sign that something isn't right.

Don't fidget with your fingers and hands. Another telltale sign that you are not truthful or at least are nervous about a specific situation is how you deal with your hands. When we keep our hands still or when we are talking and we move our hands, we are showing emotion and confidence. If however we are sitting still and we are tapping our fingers, biting our nails or just moving our hands up and down our clothing, it shows others that we are not confident and are nervous.

There are many subtle signs when it comes to body language. When we take the time to learn all of these subtle movements and non-movements, we can begin to build a picture of the internal conversations we are all having.

Don't Interrupt

When it comes to communication, it is vital that we both listen as well as speak. When we are in the middle of a conversation, it is considered rude to interrupt those who are speaking. If however you need to interject a point or make a statement, you will either want to wait for the other person to finish speaking or use your body language to signal that you would like to speak. The most common way to do this is to raise your hand or point a finger into the air.

Think Before You Speak

We have mentioned this several times throughout the book. As humans, our first instinct is to chime in on conversations and give our opinions. This can however cause more problems than they are worth. This is why it is very important to take a moment before speaking, choose the words that you want to say carefully and then speak in clear concise sentences.

Listen Well

The key to understanding the conversation is to listen well. One of the biggest mistakes we make when communicating with others is to jump into the middle of the conversation not knowing all of the facts or even what the point of the conversation is all about. The best way to avoid these problems is to keep your mouth shut, listen to what everyone else has to say before making your statements.

Never be Aggressive or Defensive

This goes back to the point of keeping our emotions in check. When we speak, we tend to dig deep down into our emotional selves. When we draw from our emotions, we tend to speak first rather than sit back and think of the words that come out of our mouths.

This form of communication will end up causing you more problems than they are worth. Another reason you don't want to be aggressive or defensive is that when we are calm and collected, we tend to get our points across better than if we were combative. If you were to be in a conversation where every idea or statement that you made was challenged or told was wrong, how would you react? For the majority of people reading this book, you would probably just want to keep your mouth shut and walk away from the conversation.

When we act in this fashion, we will never elicit change. In fact, when we act this way, people will not want to include us in the decision making process and more than likely make decisions on their own. So, when it comes to aggression and defensive attitudes, you want to keep them in check. They will do more harm than good.

Don't Deviate

Another thing that you will want to do when communicating with others is stay the course and don't deviate from your original thoughts. This is a huge issue when trying to get your point across to some people.

When you have a specific issue that you want to talk about, you don't want to jump all around the board. For example, if you are stating that you are pro in the conversation, you don't want to start making comments that are negative or go against your initial points.

When we don't deviate and are confident in our initial statements, people will take our words more seriously. If however we jump around and talk about a million different things, then people will get confused and our initial meaning as well as our own train of thought will become muddled.

Be Confident in Your Ideas

Another thing that you will want to do is make sure that you have confidence in your ideas and the points that you want to communicate. When we have an idea such as how to make a product better or how to get more customers into the store, we need to make sure that we are confident in this train of thought. When we go into a situation and make a statement, people will listen to this statement and begin to process what you said. For example, if you said, "I think we should have a half off sale this weekend in order to bring in more customers."

Once this statement is made, people will begin to process what it is that you have said and begin to form questions that will be either for that idea, against the idea or both. When this occurs, you need to be confident in your statement and be able to process what the best response will be. If you make this statement and end up having no concept on how to implement it or ways to improve upon it, then people will look at you clueless and look for some form of direction to make your idea a reality. If, however, you can support your idea, then you will have a better chance to making it a reality instead of someone else taking over the concept and turning the idea into their own.

Be Open to Feedback

Not everything that we think or say will be considered gold. In fact most people will want to interject with their own thoughts and ideas. When this happens, you must be open to it and be willing to listen to and consider all the changes. This is where most people fail in their communications.

For those who are not open to feedback are typically set in their ways. They feel that their way is the only way and if it isn't done this way, the outcome will turn out wrong. For those who are open to feedback will tend to have a greater result and build stronger bonds and relationships.

Use the Correct Communication Method

When communicating with others, it is your job to learn the best way the person you are talking to can process information. In many cases we only rely on verbal communication. This is typically the best way to communicate but it isn't the only way to communicate. In many situations communication through visual ques such as pictures, graphs, videos and even audio will help illustrate your point and will in the long run allow people to process this information in their own way.

When we take the time to use other forms of communication, we increase the likelihood that others will understand what it is we are saying and in turn can also give feedback and pointers to improving our thoughts.

End Conversations with a Hardy Handshake

The handshake is the universal greeting and farewell that people use when starting and ending conversations. When we enter a room or meet someone for the first time, we typically extend our hand out and grasp the other persons hand firmly. This sets a physical connection between the two parties. From here eye contact is engaged increasing the personal connection between the two people.

Express Yourself Using the Pronoun "I"

You will thus show your involvement in the conversation and will stand up for your positions. Choose the positive form over the negative. For example, say "Do you remember that we have a meeting tomorrow?" rather than "You haven't forgotten our meeting tomorrow morning, have you?"

Adopt Welcoming Body Language

In order to put the other person at ease, eliminate as much as possible any behavioral tics that would give away your nervousness, unease or anger (gesticulating nervously, hiding your hands in your pockets, biting your nails, etc.). The other person will then focus on your words and not on your body language.

Control Your Emotions

Whatever the situation (negative feedback, an unpleasant

remark from a colleague, etc.), do not show yourself to be too aggressive or defensive as this will not lead to any positive solution. Take a step back, try to understand the other person and, if necessary, calmly explain what is bothering you in order to ease the tension.

Establish Trusting Relationships Around You

Act with kindness to encourage your colleagues to do the same. Likewise, denounce and condemn any abusive, sexist, racist or humiliating behavior. These behaviors are unacceptable within any community and can lead to the resignation, and even burnout, of some employees.

Adapt Yourself to the Other Person

Pay attention to their verbal and body language. If they are tactile, hug them; if they are visual, illustrate your speech with the help of concrete examples; if they are more auditory, choose oral communication over written; etc. Furthermore, adjust your way of expressing yourself according to whether you are addressing your manager or a direct colleague.

Organize Internal Open Door Days

In order to encourage exchanges and to reinforce collaboration between departments, introduce your colleagues to the internal functioning so that everybody is aware of the processes and roles of each service. This will considerably reduce misunderstandings and discrepancies.

Develop an Internal Network

The internal network represents a bank of information and knowledge that is interesting and beneficial for the whole company. It invites employees to discuss specific aspects (rather than general content that nobody consults) from time to time. For example, a department could create a journal describing their daily activities which would make the work of the department in charge of taking over the project in the medium to long term much easier. You can also create a social network for the company. Based on classic social networking models, it offers employees the chance to exchange, publish information or quickly communicate with each other. This will reinforce their cohesion.

Set Specific Times for Communicating

So as to not disturb or break the concentration of the people to whom you are talking at all hours of the day, organize information meetings and interviews if you need time with a particular person. Do not forget to let them know early enough by indicating what it is about. If you only have to explain a particular detail, try to talk over coffee or during the lunch break.

Choose Between Collective or One-on-one Meetings

Depending on the type of information to be delivered. If you have to remind an employee of the rules following inappropriate behavior, there is no point involving the whole company. Following collective meetings, make a report of the decisions made available to inform those who are interested (present or absent).

Establish a Relaxation Space to Encourage Informal Exchanges

This will improve professional relationships and the atmosphere of your team. Shorter or informal meetings can also take place there.

When engaging in a handshake, a set amount of pressure is exerted on the hands. This is a telltale sign between two people and sometimes sets the tone for dominance. For instance, if one hand exerts more pressure than the others, the one with the most pressure is considered to be the more dominant person. Depending on the mental state of the individuals involved, this could set the entire tone for the conversation as well as the tone for the overall relationship.

Counter Points

When communicating with others, it is a good idea to develop a set of counter points to inject into the conversation. When we have counter points, we can say, "If they say this, we will say that." When we do this, it keeps others on their toes and you in control of the conversation.

Write Down Everything

One of the best ways to learn to communicate as well as other things is life is to write them down. When we write things down, we are more apt to remember them. One thing that you can do when writing things down is to write short stories. These short stories will put you in control of the actions and inactions of others.

For example, if you start with two characters in a room. In this room they have a box that needs to be opened. What you can do is start out by writing the conversation that each person would have. You can then jump into writing about the inner dialogue that each person is having. You can talk about what they are thinking compared to what they actually say. You can talk about their body language, their fears, hopes and desires.

At the end of the story you can conclude it with different endings. For example, could the box be a birthday or Christmas present? Who gave the present to this individual and what is their relationship status?

When we write down these stories, we can begin to train our brains to react and even anticipate actions and events that may occur in real life. If you are having trouble coming up with a story or a plot, just go back to a time in your life when you had a conversation with someone that didn't go well. Start writing down what happened exactly, how it occurred in real life and then make marks in the story where you wish you had made a different decision or choice. From there you can flesh out the story and make it your own. Then the next time you find yourself in this situation or a similar situation, you can craft the real life story to reach your intended outcome.

Chapter 18: How to Improve Communication Skills at the Workplace

The most successful people who eventually go on to become leaders and managers in the workplace are the ones who can make great impressions on everyone they work with because of how well they communicate. Of course, being able to do the job well does play a part of it as well, but when you can meaningfully and effectively communicate with the people you work with, you are already halfway towards success.

One way you can improve your communication skills is knowing what it is you really want to say and why you want to say it. You'll have a hard time saying something that you're not sure you want to say. Knowing the reason for saying it is equally important because it helps you figure out the best words and tone of voice to use in communicating that which you really want to communicate. If you can also learn more about who you're communicating with, you'll increase your chances of being able to clearly communicate to that person.

Another way of improving your communication skills is considering how you'll communicate that which you want to. One of the best communicators I've read about is Jesus Christ. Religious or not, you can appreciate His use of parables as a way of illustrating relatively deep spiritual truths. He already knew ahead of time that stories help people learn spiritual or moral lessons better.

But you can't use parables to communicate a scientific finding resulting from a series of controlled experiments. For such, you'll need more numbers than stories.

Listening is another way to communicate better. How? When you listen better, you'll be able to know the other person or the audience better. When you do, you'll know what to communicate and how to communicate better in ways that they'll really understand.

Chapter 19: Working Relationships

Good communication within the workplace fosters a better working environment that is more conducive to employee productivity. With effective communication guidelines in place, employees will understand expectations. There will be ongoing discussions of strategies and resolutions. This creates a more goal-oriented team that will be more productive. Better communication in the workplace also means better relationships among employees. A more satisfying work experience can also drive productivity and increase the employee retention rate.

The majority of misunderstandings or miscommunications in the workplace stem from a lack of effective communication. The use of empathic listening and assertive speaking in the workplace can nearly eliminate these misunderstandings, and also provide a framework for conflict resolution. Empathic listening can make a real difference in every workplace from meeting rooms to factory floors to classrooms. Its consistent use among employees, managers, and clients will decrease the potential for misunderstandings and create an overall better working experience for all involved.

Practical Exercise to Improve Communication in Working Relationships

A good training tool for effective communication in the workplace is the **empathy circle**. An empathy circle gives employees the chance to practice empathic listening and (with time) make it more organic for the workplace culture. The following is a description of how an empathy circle works.

Empathy circles work best with a group of four participants. When working with a larger company, the group can be broken down into smaller clusters for this exercise to take place.

Within each small group, each member is assigned a role. The first member will be the speaker, the next member will be the active listener, and the remaining members will be silent listeners.

It is best to have a topic ready to assign to the groups. You may also wish to assign a side for each group member to take on the assigned topic.

The person who is assigned the role of speaker begins to talk about the topic to the active listener. The speaker and active listener should maintain eye contact throughout this part of the exercise. The active listener listens until the speaker feels fully understood. The active listener should not interrupt or pass judgment, but may ask for clarification if needed or try to make a restatement to the speaker to ensure understanding. The silent listeners only listen at this point and observe the interactions between the speaker and the listener.

At the time that the speaker feels completely understood, it is time to switch roles. The active listener becomes the new speaker. A new topic may be assigned at this time. The former speaker now becomes a silent listener and one of the silent listeners takes on the role of active listener.

This exercise continues until each person has had a chance to play each role. In closing out this exercise, there should be time allotted for employees to give thoughts and make observations about how this type of effective communication will work better for the company.

Chapter 20: What Barriers Prohibit Effective Workplace Communication

During the communication process, there are sometimes barriers which tend to come up that can result in poor communication. These are known as communication barriers, and these are the reasons your messages become misunderstood, taken out of context or even distorted. To overcome these communication barriers, you must first understand what they are.

While effective communication in a workplace is essential, there are factors that prevent employers and employees from its benefits. For example, the bigger the company, the more complex communication issues will be. However, let me point out that the basic principles of communication are applicable to all businesses, whether large or small. Among the most common communication problems in companies are the use of wrong communication methods, misunderstandings and failure to confirm whether the message was received and understood.

People who work in upper and middle management must check

the level of awareness, understanding and concern among their subordinates before communicating messages. Employees don't know or need to know all things happening in the company. However, there are issues about which they need to be informed, mainly because it concerns them. Companies should also check the level of understanding of its workers about any issues concerning the company, ensuring that any gaps are bridged with effective communication right away.

Modern technology has allowed people to communicate faster, but not necessarily more efficiently. Businesses today benefit a great deal from various methods of communication. The problem lies in choosing and using the appropriate channels for the messages. Companies must know which communication channels are best for the type of message, their target audience and the situation. Some messages can be relayed best through a face-to-face meeting while some are most effectively disseminated through an email, a chat message or an SMS. It will also greatly depend on the importance of the message to be relayed. The more important the message is, the more important it is to have a face-to-face meeting. One good example is the firing of an employee. Another example is a school has chosen to post its graduation announcements and updates through its Twitter and Facebook accounts; unfortunately, not all the school's students have Twitter or Facebook accounts. Moreover, not all of those who have accounts in these social networking sites regularly check their Facebook and Twitter pages. The communication channels used by the school are not effective or useful for all students. On the other hand, if the school limited all its information dissemination to its bulletin boards, the students would need to go to the school grounds daily to check for new updates. Companies should put an effort into determining the most appropriate communication channels in order to relay messages more efficiently.

There are also physical barriers to effective workplace communication. Many modern work stations have eliminated cubicles that separate workers. Instead, there is an open space that allows people to communicate more freely. However, recent studies have shown that open offices have reduced productivity, as employees are unhappy about the lack of privacy, noise, opportunities for gossiping and inability to concentrate on their daily tasks. Other barriers to effective workplace communication can include differences in personality. For instance, shy, introverted people tend not to speak with anyone unnecessarily, but keep to themselves and just be a loner. Low self-esteem can also prevent people from communicating effectively to their coworkers. People's differences may prevent effective workplace communication, but good companies can have all kinds of training made available to their employees in order to help them become more effective communicators. Company owners and leaders who understand the power of effective communication know that a workforce with the ability to effectively communicate can bring more business to the company.

Communication is a complex matter. Whether in your everyday life or at work, misinterpretation sometimes does happen in communication. Sometimes, even with the best intentions, it is unavoidable. Messages may not come across or be received in the way that we intended which is why it is important to understand the causes of communication barriers and what can be done to overcome them.

Time

Make a rule to be punctual always and attend meetings on time. If you are the host and need to present a topic, it is a good practice to reach the meeting venue 15-20 minutes prior to make sure everything required for the meeting is available.

Discomfort with the topic

If you are the speaker and going to talk about a difficult topic/decision (for e.g. changes to policies, implementation of new rules, company decisions and so on), you will most likely face a group that is dissatisfied or negative about the decision. This can often make the communication one way or make way for heated arguments when people take a defensive approach.

Language differences

Different languages come with different accents, and sometimes, difficulty understanding a person's accent can also be a communication barrier. Perhaps they may be pronouncing certain words differently, or the way their sentences run together may be difficult to understand because of a thick accent for example.

Using jargon

Not everyone may be familiar with certain jargon, and sometimes these unfamiliar terms can cause confusion and complicate things for the person who is trying to understand your message.

Making assumptions

A common communication barrier, this frequently occurs when someone decides to reach a decision or course of action without fully listening to all the information at hand. Making assumptions can lead to complications because when you are not well informed, you run the risk of making more mistakes than you should.

Lack of attention

Not paying full attention is considered a communication barrier. Sometimes, our mind tends to wander or drift when someone else is talking. Or we may be the ones who are doing the talking, but we run the risk of losing the other person's interest because the topic doesn't rivet them enough. When attention starts to drift, it can be easy to miss crucial points in the message.

Distractions

Imagine you are in the middle of an important conversation with someone, but all around you, there are all sorts of distractions. General noise, other people talking, phones ringing, traffic honking, messages beeping into your mobile phone, even the urge to frequently check social media is a distraction. All of these distractions can also be a communication barrier because it makes it harder to focus on your communication with another person. It makes it harder for them to fully pay attention to what you are saying too which means there is a chance that they may not fully be processing the information you are giving them.

Information overloading

One thing that everyone would do well to remember when it

comes to communication is that not everyone thinks, reacts or processes information in the same way. One person may be able to process information quickly and efficiently while another person may need more time to properly digest that same piece of information. Individuals are unique in the way that they function and operate, and therefore, information overloading can sometimes be seen as a communication barrier. If, for example, you deliver information too much too soon, you may run the risk of overwhelming the receiver, and as a result, they may not be able to fully process or understand what it is that you are trying to convey.

Current emotional state

There may be times when it isn't necessarily the best time to bring up a certain subject or topic of discussion. Emotions such as sadness, anger, nervousness, and distractions or frustration can hamper the way messages are communicated or received. If someone is not in the right frame of mind or state to pay full attention to what you have to say, they may not be able to process that message appropriately. Similarly, if you are not in the right frame of mind to communicate your message effectively because you are not in a calm and focused state, for example, you may not be able to communicate your message as effectively as you should.

Lack of confidence

Lacking confidence is also viewed as a communication barrier. When a speaker lacks the necessary confidence needed, they become shy and find it difficult to assert themselves properly, making it difficult to convey messages or make their opinions known. Lacking confidence can result in a lot of awkward pauses, stammering, and stuttering which could garble the messages and prevent them from being communicated effectively.

Rushing through the message

Never convey messages in a rushed or hasty manner. Doing this puts you at risk of missing out crucial information that needs to be communicated, and your listener could miss out on possible information too because they're unable to keep up with what you may be saying. Rushing through messages is never a good idea unless you have the time to spare for a proper discussion, so don't do it.

How to Overcome These Communication Barriers

Now that you know the type of barriers which can occur that prevent effective communication from happening, here comes the next question. How do we overcome these barriers? Luckily, for every problem, there is a solution, even when it comes to effective communication.

Here are some strategies you can employ to improve your communication with your peers:

Take steps to clarify

To help improve the effectiveness of your message going across, spend sometimes clarifying the message that you want to communicate before you communicate it. If it helps, write down what you want to say as it makes it easier to assess your message when you see it written down in front of you. To help you determine if your message is clear enough, ask yourself is the objective of the message clear, ask yourself if you are getting all the important information across, and analyze which aspect of the message could be misunderstood and what you can do to prevent that from happening.

Communicate with your receiver in mind

Messages sometimes need to be adjusted and tweaked a little bit depending on whom you are talking to. Remember that people tend to process information differently? You wouldn't necessarily communicate a certain message to your boss the same way that you would to your colleague or a friend. The way you talk and your approach would be completely different. When preparing to communicate, to ensure that your message is the most effective, you need to structure and prepare it according to who is going to receive the message. Making it easier to understand for the receiver improves your chances of that message being communicated effectively.

Keep the language and tone in mind

When attempting to communicate your messages, you – as the communicator – need to ensure that you frame those messages in a clear, easy to understand language. You also need to be aware of the tone you use to deliver that message. Ideally, it should be in a manner that will not risk offending or injuring the feelings of the receiver. The language used to deliver those messages should also be kept brief, concise and to the point. Avoid using unnecessary jargon or technical terms where possible because those could just overcomplicate things.

Get some feedback

The best way to find out if your message was communicated effectively enough is to ask your audience directly. Feedback can go a long way in helping you determine what needs to be improved or whether your messages were clear and easy to understand. After you have delivered your message, before you end your conversation, ask your recipient in a friendly manner if everything was okay and do they need any further clarification on any matters.

Keep your messages consistent

When communicating, you need to take extra measures to ensure that your messages remain consistent and your points don't contradict each other. What you are trying to convey should be consistent and with a clear focus in mind so as not to confuse your recipient. When communicating at work, ensure that your messages are clearly in line with the company's objectives, mission, and policies so your colleagues or employees are clear on what needs to be done.

Listening effectively

Being able to listen effectively is also part of the effective communication process. Both the communicator and the receiver must be able to listen effectively to one another while each is expressing their points of view. Relevant and important information is in danger of being missed if you are not able to listen well to what the communicator is trying to say to you. And in the case of the communicator, they would also need to be able to listen to the feedback that they are receiving if they hope to improve their communication skills moving forward.

Minimize distraction

To avoid your messages being lost in translation, finding a good place where you can conduct a discussion is going to be your best bet. Another way to minimize distraction is to turn off mobile devices (one of the main causes of distraction today, especially among the millennials). Remove the source of the distraction. The less the distraction, the higher the chances of improved concentration and focus when a discussion is taking place thereby improving effective communication.

Using the right word selection

Word selection is important in determining how effective your messages come across. Words are the source of facilitating effective communication, and careless or improper use of words are usually the reason for poor communication. To improve the effectiveness of your communication, start by carefully considering the types of words used in delivering your message. Minimize the use of jargon, slang and overly technical terms which may not necessarily be understood by your receiver. What you can do, instead, is to opt for common and familiar words, single words which deliver the point across more concisely instead of several words, and use shorter words where possible instead of longer phrases. The more concise and succinct your message, the easier it is to understand.

Focus on what you are trying to say

Stay focused on the message you are trying to get your receiver to understand, and avoid steering the direction of the conversation into unrelated territory. For example, at the workplace, if you were talking about a coworker's performance, focus on the performance aspect alone and avoid discussing unrelated matters such as their personality or the way they are dressed as an example. The more you stay focused on the subject at hand, the better you can ensure that the point of the discussion is clearly communicated with no mixed messages in between.

Avoid inflicting an air of superiority

Whether you are discussing something with your friends or your coworkers, even if you feel that you are well versed and more knowledgeable about the subject at hand, do not inflict an air of superiority when you are having a discussion. Be relatable and talk to your receiver like an equal, because this helps them be more receptive and attentive to the things you have to say.

Using visuals

This step is more appropriate for meetings or presentations

conducted at work. Instead of droning on and on, and at risk of losing the attention of your audience, try including some message-related visuals into your presentation. Not only will this help break the monotony, but you will continue to hold the attention of your audience, improving the chances of your message getting across.

Communication barriers will happen from time to time, whether we like it or not. Whether in everyday life or the workplace, effective communication makes a difference in the way you convey yourself and how easily you are understood by others around you. The way it works is simple – the easier you are to understand, the better your chances of achieving success in whatever task you are undertaking at the moment.

The best thing to do in this instance to prevent the message from being misunderstood or distorted is to be aware of the situation in which you are holding your communication session, and do your best to minimize the effects wherever possible. Effective communication is possible, once you have a better understanding of what you can do to encourage it.

Chapter 21: Workplace Communication Techniques

Through certain communication techniques, effective workplace communication can be attained. Communication skills are very important and business owners are aware that it is necessary for their business to progress. Employers and employees need to interact with each other on a daily basis, and the ability to communicate well cannot be overemphasized. Effective communication in the workplace helps people create good professional relationships. When people in a company have good communication skills, the needs of the company and the workers are fully met. Here are some communication techniques that one can try in order to communicate more effectively:

Define your objective.

What is your purpose for communicating? Do you need to sell something, influence or persuade your listener, or do you just need to inform? If you determine the purpose of your communication and have a clear goal in mind, then you can communicate to your audience more effectively.

Know your audience.

You have a certain advantage when you understand your audience. For example, if you are aware of cultural differences between Americans and Asians, then you can find ways to communicate better to your Asian coworkers. At the same time, if you know that your boss has certain preferences and dislikes, you can use this knowledge in your communication. Knowing what your customers need allows you to communicate more effectively and provide better service.

Choose the best communication channels.

The communication channel that you use should be the best for your audience, not for you. For instance, it is more convenient for you to just text updates to your subordinates. You know that they will have questions, but you still choose this method instead of calling for a face-to-face meeting. Communication channels should also fit your purpose.

Prepare your key points.

It will be easier for you to deliver your message if you have an outline and categorize it from the most important to the least important points. In addition, your listeners can better absorb the information you are sharing when it is organized. Whether you have to communicate with a group or just one-on-one, it helps to organize your main points. This also eliminates the possibility for speakers to talk endlessly in a directionless manner.

Ask if your audience understood your message.

After delivering your message, always make it a point to know whether the audience understood what you said. Provide more explanation and information if you were not clear. Check for any misinterpretations and be sure to correct any errors. Repeat the message if necessary. Communication is not effective if nobody understands you so make sure that your message is clear and understood.

Through these simple communication techniques, you can become a more effective communicator. Effective communication in the workplace can be achieved and everyone can have a more satisfying working experience when there are fewer misunderstandings and fewer problems caused by poor communication.

Chapter 22: How to Become a Brilliant Public Speaker

Here are proven tips and strategies you can use to become a powerful and brilliant public speaker.

Regulate Your Tone

To become an impactful speaker and a great storyteller, make good use of your voice. You must increase and decrease its pitch and speed when necessary. If you want to emphasize an important point, speak in a strong and loud tone, and lower it when expressing disappointment. Adding emotions to your speech helps you become an effective storyteller and helps you connect with your audience.

Work on Nonverbal Communication

Public speaking is not just about speaking. It comprises both verbal and nonverbal communication. To influence your audience, become good at both verbal and nonverbal communication. To master nonverbal communication, effectively use your expressions and body language.

Firstly, look your audience directly in the eye. Direct eye contact supercharges your confidence and proves you know what you are saying which makes people agree with you.

Secondly, keep your body straight, but not tight and firm. Your body posture needs to be correct and you must sit or stand straight. However, your body must not be stiff because stiffness is a sign of insecurity.

Thirdly, change your expressions from time to time depending on the tone and message of your speech. For instance, if the topic is grim and serious, your expression needs to be serious as well. The emotions on your face show your seriousness about the topic and help the audience understand your concern.

Fourthly, make proper use of appropriate hand gestures throughout your speech. Thump your fist on the podium when showing determination or make a fist pump when encouraging your crowd to do something. Hand gestures add feelings to your speech and help the audience enjoy it.

Research Your Audience

To connect with your audience, you need to give them what they want. To do that, you need to write a compelling speech comprising all the information your audience wants. This is where audience research comes in handy.

Before drafting your speech, you MUST always research your audience, their interests, age group, gender, knowledge level regarding your topic, and profession. This helps you prepare your speech according to their respective needs and demands which allows you to offer your audience precisely what they need.

Focus on the 3 C's

To make your speech powerful, focus on the three C's. Your message needs to be clear, concise, and consistent. Make sure you use the right set of words to convey your message and ensure your message does not exceed more than it needs to be.

For instance, if a point becomes clear in 100 words, do not add another 100 just to prove your knowledge. People actually hate lengthy speeches and consider it a waste of their precious time. Keep your message as succinct, clear, and ensure consistency throughout your speech. When you take care of these three, you will draft an impeccable speech.

Showing You Are Approachable

Your audience should never get the feeling you are not approachable because not being approachable means you are haughty; the audience hates haughty speakers. To charm your audience and connect with them, make them feel you are approachable. Ask them to consult you during your working hours and encourage them to contact you whenever needed, especially if you are a motivational speaker. You must also smile at your audience and speak politely so they can easily talk to you without feeling too hesitant.

Use the Space Well

Make good use of space when presenting your topic. If you have a big stage that you can walk on, then make sure to walk a little after speaking for a few minutes. Walking around the stage reflects your confidence whereas standing still in one spot is a symbol of nervousness.

Prepare Activities

If you have an hour or two to speak on a topic, prepare interactive activities for your audience and invite their suggestions and queries at the end of your speech. This helps your speech become entertaining and interactive for your listeners.

Add in Quotes, Facts, Statistics, and Metaphors

Do add in appropriate quotes, metaphors, statistics, and facts that relate to your speech wherever you deem suitable. These elements add more structure and substance to your speech, giving it an authoritative appeal which in turn can help you influence your addressees easily.

Build Your Credibility

You always must extensively research a topic before speaking on it so you can answer all the queries thrown your way by your addressees. However, if you are unable to answer a question, you must accept your inadequacy and apologize to the questioner for not satisfying his or her query at that particular moment. Tell the questioner you will research the question and offer answers when you do. Ask the questioner to leave his or her email address with you. When you do find a reasonable answer to the question, respond so you can build and enhance your credibility.

In addition to following the above tips, implement all the strategies discussed in this guide, especially those related to confidence and persuasion skills as to become a remarkable public speaker, you need these two skills.

Chapter 23: Necessary Information

The first and most important part of communication in the workplace is identifying important information. Important information is the who, what, where, when, why, and how of a relevant situation. Workplace communication should always cover all of these questions even if the answer is currently unknown. Not knowing one of these elements if very often far more important than knowing all of the others.

For example, say you are working in a manufacturing environment. The production scheduler has sent out an email stating that 300 cases of widgets need to be produced. This email really only gives the "what" of the situation: 300 cases of widgets need to be produced. It does not cover who will make them, where they will be produced, when they are needed, why they are needed, or how they are to be made. With this basic bit of information, it may very well be accomplished by the production department due to their knowledge of the missing information. However, each of these missing pieces of information is an opportunity for miscommunication leading to a problem.

What if two separate production operations are performed? Well, then you have 600 cases of widgets and a lot of wasted time and money. What if they add this order to the end of their current log? Shipping dates could be missed, because no one knew that it was a rush order. What if the product is new and instructions have not been developed. Production will most likely encounter delays while trying to assemble something for the first time.

It may seem unnecessary to spell things out. It may even seem like you are talking down to your coworkers. Telling people things you think they should already know is part of good communication though. One way to avoid missing information is to establish a clear template for your communications. Each communication is then formatted in a way that can be checked for completeness. This is one reason why forms are such an important tool in any business environment.

Forms

Forms are one of the most overlooked, least appreciated methods of communication in a workplace. They are often viewed by employees and customers either as a hassle or, at best, an afterthought. In reality these should be a way to clearly and consistently communicate vital information within an organization. Forms build the framework for how communication will flow from start to finish.

When developing forms, it is important to include input from everyone who will fill out, use, or review the information on the form. Many times the responsible group will design a form to their specifications without consulting other departments. This can lead to using specialized jargon that other groups do not know or leaving off needed information that is not used by the group developing the form.

Forms should always be as concise as possible while still incorporating all of the needed information. Extra information is not bad, but unnecessary information distracts from the purpose of the form. Each form should have a specific purpose and fulfill one task, communicating the necessary information from one group to another regarding an activity. The information fields on a form should also be titled clearly in plain language and should provide anyone who is given the form all of the needed information to fill out or interpret the information on the form. The blank form is also an opportunity for good or poor communication.

A good form should be able to achieve its purpose without any additional or outside communication. The information on the form should communicate everything the receiving group needs to perform their tasks. If a form does not contain all of this information, then it should be revised to include it. Creating an informal communication chain is not a reliable solution to an incomplete or confusing form.

Everyone who comes into contact with a form should receive training on how to fill out and read the form. Training should be done as a group so that all questions can be addressed together. This is important to ensure that the language of the form is clear and that there will not be miscommunication due to differences in terminology.

A well-developed form can last forever, but every form should be constantly evaluated and revised as needed. Likewise, the performance of those using the form should be evaluated and additional training conducted to increase communication accuracy and eliminate gaps in information sharing. Just like other operations and processes within an organization, communication should be continuously monitored for improvement opportunities.

Once a form is completed and all necessary actions are completed, the form should be dispositioned according to the need for reviewing the information on the form. This end of life stage is often forgotten when designing a form. Determining how the form will be filed, where it will be kept, and how long it will be maintained are all just as important as what is on the form itself.

Forms should be kept for as long as anyone may need to review the information recorded on it. Some types of information have legal requirements for how long they must be held or when they must be destroyed. These regulations always trump the organization's opinions. If there are no regulations for the form, then the organization can create a disposition schedule. A good rule is to keep the form for twice as long as anyone thinks they will need it.

Emails

Most communication in the modern business world is done through emails. These communications range from short informal notes to lengthy formal memorandums. When communicating information, it is best to pick one format and stick to it. If you put the same information in the same places every time, then the people you are communicating with will learn to anticipate the information you are sending. This not only helps them to understand what you are trying to share with them, but it will also empower them to ask for clarification if something looks different. That is what makes good communication: active engagement from all participants.

Do not skimp on the Subject line or use generic terminology. Be specific about what the subject of the email is about. If it is a recurring email, then include a date in the subject line. This subject line will serve as a key piece of filing information and will help make the email easier to locate if anyone needs to retrieve it later on. Using a tag (i.e. [Project Name], URGENT, etc.) at the beginning can also help. Also, do not continue email threads past the conclusion of the original topic. Create a new email to address the new topic so that it does not get lost in another email chain.

Emails should never be too short to contain all the necessary information. There is no shortage of pixels or storage space in modern computer systems. Take the time to craft your emails carefully and make sure that all of the needed information is contained in your first email. Nothing is as frustrating as asking questions via email and only getting partial or incomplete responses. Having to repeat yourself in a conversation is never a sign of good communication.

One of the best practices to follow is to put the bottom line up front. This BLUF method allows you to get straight to the point of a lengthy email. Also, most people will see a preview of the text in the email before they open it. Having the most important information at the top of the email means that it is more likely to be displayed in the preview. A BLUF should be a quick one sentence thesis statement that gets across the topic and urgency of the email.

Like forms, emails should be filed. You should be saving your emails where you can find important emails wherever you go. Most email services can travel with you anywhere in the world. One exception is the archive file that many people with heavy email traffic create on their desktops. If you are saving your emails in this way, then bear in mind that these emails will not travel with you if you access your email on a different device. It is better to keep your important emails in an online location whenever possible.

Conversations

Talking to people may seem old fashioned to some, but it is still a major form of communication. Many times important matters necessitate a real time conversation whether it be a teleconference, a phone call, or a face-to-face meeting. These conversations should be tackled with the most care. There is no greater opportunity for miscommunication than talking with another person.

Human beings have a great propensity for saying or hearing the wrong things. When compared to written communications, oral communication is far more complex. It is more than just what words you choose to say, but how you say them and what your body is doing as you say them. Furthermore, your listener is interpreting your words in real-time while also thinking about their responses at the same exact time and there is nothing you can do about it.

The best option you have is to over communicate during a conversation. It may irritate some of your coworkers, but it will ensure better understanding. Ask for clarifications and understanding. Assumptions are famous for the ability to complicate situations. Think about what assumptions you are bringing into a conversation and challenge them by asking the questions to confirm or dispel them. Also, think about what assumptions the other parties might be bringing with them and clarify what information you are trying to share. In the worst case scenario, you are all already on the same page and you will have confirmed it.

Any verbal communication should be followed up in writing. If someone calls you with an urgent question on the phone, then follow up with an email after you hang up. This way you can document the conversation in a format that you can bring up later. It may also address an assumption that was made during the phone call. Again, verbal communication can be tricky and following up with a clearly formatted written communication can help avoid miscommunication.

If someone tries to go around an established form by talking to you directly, then it is important that they be directed to fill out the form at the end of the conversation. Oftentimes there is no harm in asking questions or sharing information verbally, but circumventing established procedures is never the right path. You should firmly, but politely remind them that there is a form for the information they are trying to communicate and offer to assist them with finding and filling out the form.

If a conversation becomes repeated enough to warrant a form, then take the initiative to begin creating one. Information that is routinely being communicated warrants a form. It can save time and avoid extra questions. Plus, it will automatically be captured in writing and filed appropriately.

Chapter 24: Unnecessary Information

Communication channels are not infinitely broad. There is a limit to how much information can effectively be conveyed. So, it is just as important to leave out unnecessary information as it is to include the necessary information.

First, we must look at common pieces of information included in communication that are unnecessary. These include errors, assumptions, and judgments. Each of these can cause confusion and harm within communication channels. This harm can go beyond the specific communication and can actually harm professional relationships within the workplace.

Errors

Errors can be found in any form of communication and are often inserted accidentally. The communicator may mistype, misspeak, or simply enter information in sloppy handwriting. Sometimes these errors will be caught by the recipients and only serve to slow down the communication process by forcing them to seek clarification or corrections. Other times these errors can slip by and cause serious problems.

Every communication should follow a set format whenever possible not only to ensure the inclusion of the necessary information, but also to help highlight any anomalies caused by errors. Again the simple form is a great tool for avoiding miscommunications when designed and implemented properly. However, even forms can generate errors and that is why training and evaluation are so important.

You should also proofread any written communications that you prepare to check for errors. If something does not look correct, then double check it before you send off the form or email. Spending this time double checking yourself may save others the time of having to double check your work.

This should include grammar and spelling checks. Even if you think you are getting your point across, your professional communication should be as grammatically correct as possible. The rules of grammar and spelling are there to create a common baseline for how we communicate. Upholding these rules is a core component to building effective communication channels.

When speaking, make sure you are listening to what you are saying and do not be afraid to slow down and think about what you are saying. It is not uncommon to begin speaking more quickly when a problem arises or when tensions are high. These situations are when accuracy can really matter the most. Taking the time to say the correct thing will save time in the long run.

Remember that mistakes speak louder than anything. Each error you make in your communications will outweigh a hundred correct pieces of information. This is especially true the further that error traveled before it was caught. Take the time to check your information not just for your recipients, but for your own reputation.

Assumptions

These assumptions can be even more harmful than the unspoken variety. The more forcefulness or confidence that is put behind them the worse. Never assume that something is correct, always get confirmation. Especially, do not make assumptions regarding individuals or groups who are not included in the conversation you are having. Since, they are not there to set the record straight, these assumptions will most likely go uncontested and uncorrected allowing them to continue on spreading throughout the organization. When they do finally reach the affected person or group you can safely assume that you will hear about it.

Just like double checking your communications for errors, look over your communications for assumptions. Examine each piece of information you are presenting and ask yourself, "How do I know this?" If you cannot answer the question, then you need to do some more research or rephrase your telling of the information as asking for confirmation. Do not be afraid to admit that you do not know for certain what the correct information is. It is better to admit your ignorance than to communicate possibly inaccurate information with undue confidence.

The most harmful assumptions that you can communicate are those that seem the least likely to be assumptions. These are often couched in surrounding or even supporting facts. If you are listing out necessary information to answer the questions of who, what, where, when, why, and how and you need to add in some unconfirmed information, make it abundantly clear. Use style changes or emphasis to draw attention to the information or expressly proclaim it as possibly incorrect information. Do not assume that others will know when you are making an assumption.

Judgements

We all make judgements every day. It is part of life and it is part of our jobs. There is nothing wrong with making judgements, but how we communicate them is important. Not every communication needs to include judgements and often they are unnecessary when trying to share information.

Judgements tend to engage people differently than information. People will quickly become defensive if they feel like the judgements are directed at them and defensive coworkers do not make the best communication partners. That is why it is important to engage others within your organization without making judgements.

For example, if you need to communicate that a project is delayed, do not assign blame. Stick to the facts of the situation and make sure to clarify if any assumptions are included in what you are sharing. Phrasing these unverified assumptions as questions can help to engage the recipients rather than leave them feeling attacked. The conversation about what happened or what should have happened can be had separately and with a singular focus. This is about sharing information.

Developing a reputation as a judgmental coworker is not good for communications. The more this reputation is developed, the more judgmental any of your communication will be perceived. After a while, people may put up their defenses as soon as they see you or read your name on an email. This will make it very hard for you to engage them meaningfully in the future and can be very hard to undo. If you feel like this is happening, then you need to make sure you are extra careful in your communication and be sure to address any time you feel your recipients are becoming defensive. **Do not avoid the topic. The only way the air will get cleared is if you clear it.**

Other Unnecessary Information

Other unnecessary information could be literally anything. Do not clutter up communication channels with unrelated or unprofessional information. Even if it is work related, if it is not relevant to the conversation, it should not be shared there. Create a separate communication. This could mean creating a new form, writing a new email, or finishing the current conversation before switching topics.

Never spread gossip, rumors, or personal information through official work channels. I do not personally recommend spreading them at all, but if you must, then do so through your personal communication channels. These topics have no place in professional communications.

Chapter 25: Choosing Your Audience

The need to communicate should always begin with information that needs to be shared not with an audience to address. You are not picking a topic for a speech you must deliver, you are crafting a communication to share necessary information.

It is always best to begin each communication activity by determining who you will be communicating with. This allows you to decide how you communicate with them. Do you need a specific form? Should you schedule a meeting? Will you need the big conference room? After you have made these decisions, then you can craft truly targeted communication that will convey the information you have to share in the most effective way.

We have all received emails that do not pertain to us. Beyond even the large amounts of spam mail, we often receive messages that carry real and useful information for other people that somehow our names were included on. These emails take our time, distract us from what we are doing, and clog our communication channels. Do not continue to be a part of this problem.

Do not fall into the trap of putting everyone on that email. If you communicate everything to everyone regardless of whether or not it pertains to them, then you will only succeed in annoying them and reducing your own effectiveness. There is no benefit to sharing information that does not need to be shared either because it is unnecessary entirely or simply unnecessary to the recipient.

Likewise, do not waste your coworkers' time with meetings that do not share information they need. We all have other things we can be doing besides sitting through a meeting that does not pertain to us. If you are unsure, then approach them before the meeting to ask if it is something they need to know about. If they are unsure, invite them to attend but let them know that they may leave if they decide they do not need to be there.

Never include unnecessary people on communications that carry negative information. It is acceptable to publicize praise, but it is never okay to humiliate anyone in front of others. Admonishments, reprimands, and criticism should always be delivered as privately as possible. Not only do others not need to be distracted by these communications, but the recipients will respect your discretion and be more likely to engage in the conversation.

When starting an ongoing conversation, feel free to include any possible necessary recipients with the invitation for anyone to opt out of future communications. This way your recipients can decide on their own involvement.

Chapter 26: Other Considerations

Outside of these cardinal rules lies a whole world of opportunities to communicate or miscommunicate information. We will go over a few that I have run into consistently.

Brevity

We are all on a schedule. None of us want to waste time on unnecessary or unnecessarily long emails, phone calls, or paperwork. There is a real value to keeping things brief. Brevity does not trump effective communication though. **Remember haste makes waste.** Shooting off that two line email may have been quick, but dealing with the clarifying questions that bounce back or the fallout from not conveying all of the needed information will not.

So, how long is too long and how short is too short. Well, too short is easy. If it does not adequately answer the who, what, where, when, why and how, then you need to keep communicating. Too long is a bit harder to define. The best rule is to monitor your own interest in what you are writing or saying. If you start to lose yourself, then you probably have already lost your audience. **Always try to find the most direct way to communicate. These are professional communications not theatrics.** Hyperbole, dramatics, and long-winded speeches are not the goal here.

If you do feel like you are getting a bit long-winded in the conversation, then consider changing communication methods. Any email exchange that begins to devolve into short one or two line responses should most likely be moved to a phone call. Phone calls are great for short back and forth conversations and you can always compose an email summarizing what was talked about when you are done. If you are having a conversation and realize that other people should be involved, then it may be time to draft an email or schedule a meeting. Meetings are really great when you find yourself having to address a lot of assumptions in your communications. They allow you to provide the information you need to share and then take questions from the recipients.

Tone

How you communicate is just as important as what you are communicating. The appropriate tone will vary depending on your workplace. It is always best to default to a more professional and reserved tone. You will be better served by gaining a reputation as cold or dull than infusing too much emotion of any kind in your communications. Sometimes, though, it is appropriate to use a more informal tone to foster goodwill with your employees or coworkers. This does not mean you should be attempting to manipulate anyone, but just use the tone that the recipient will best be able to understand. Remember, you need this audience to actively engage in the conversation to ensure effective communication.

Style

Word choice is the most important part of determining your communication style. Again it is best to default to a simple, straightforward style in your communications. You need to make sure you are communicating with words that everyone should know the meaning of to avoid any misunderstandings. Sometimes, though, it is appropriate or necessary to use more complex words. Emails involving technical details are often a jumble of specialized jargon that the uninitiated would have little hope of comprehending. This is unfortunately an unavoidable part of doing business in specialized fields. Just make sure that what you are communicating will convey the appropriate meaning to everyone in your audience. This should be easy within your organization if senior leadership has cultivated a shared dialect that all the departments participate in. If you are in a fragmented organization, then you may need to know when to switch your style to meet the different dialects of the different tribes.

Confrontation

Very few people enjoy real confrontations. This can be especially tense in a work environment. It is best to take your time when crafting the message you will convey during a confrontation. Having your message prepared can give you time to soften some rough edges in your tone or style. It can also help you to refine your message. As little as anyone likes receiving criticism or reprimands, they enjoy it dragging on for an extended period of time even less.

When possible always confront people privately, but I advise against sending anything negative in an email. It is always better to use the most expressive means of communication available to avoid your recipient from placing their own perceptions on top of your words. Face to face is always my first choice for a difficult conversation. A one-on-one conversation allows you to be candid and express your message with full articulation.

Chapter 27: Effective Persuasion Techniques and Strategies

Although massive, it is advantageous to improve your persuasion skills; however, to become amazingly persuasive so that you can influence everyone you interact with, calls for some serious investment in developing the skill of persuasion.

This section focuses on helping you develop brilliant persuasion skills by outlining effective tips and tricks you can use to become incredibly convincing and swaying. Let us find out how extremely persuasive people achieve their objective.

How to Become Extremely Persuasive

To become persuasive, influence, and sway opinions:

Know the Right Time to Stop and Back Away

Successful persuaders do not constantly berate others with constant verbal garbage. Wearing your listeners down through incessant speaking is not a viable strategy. Know when to stop and back off. Showing extreme urgency when trying to influence people is never an effective tactic. You must know when your listeners need you to shut up and back away.

After making your point and providing enough information to persuade, stop and talk casually. You should even leave that room if you feel your presence might suffocate the other person. Give the individual enough breathing space and time to make his or her own decision. This clever move shows them you do not want to enforce your will; rather, you respect their opinion.

Follow all these tips and tricks and practice them as much as you can. Quite soon, you will accomplish your goal and become a fantastic persuader.

To convince others about something, you must be an expert on that topic. You need to be knowledgeable about the topic you address and know the nitty-gritty of it. People are inquisitive in nature and will seek answers to queries they do not understand. If you consistently fail to answer their questions conclusively, they will never even consider conforming to your influence. Therefore, you must completely research a topic and then address the concerned people. This is especially important when speaking at business meetings, or giving presentations to business partners, potential partners, and business associates.

When you have the full understanding of a subject, you show people you are an expert; they thus have no choice but to accept your expert opinion.

Be Purposeful

Truly convincing and influential people are extremely purposeful. They know and comprehend their power, skills, and capabilities, and use them knowingly and sparingly. They are aware that normal conversations do not revolve around getting someone to accept or do something they want. They do not aggressively push others to do something they want. Rather, they plan every move very tactfully and cleverly to get to their purpose.

To become truly persuasive, you need to become purposeful. For that, you need to bid adieu to the habit of arguing with people on different ideas and strongly advocating for your viewpoint. Say what you have to say in an amicable and calm tone, and do not push others to accept your ideas. Stay true to your idea, because there is no need to give it up but do not force others to embrace it. When people notice your calmness mixed with your persistence, they will ultimately start becoming more open to your ideas and will start accepting them.

Listen A Lot and A Little More

Yes, we have said a lot about having great listening skills; however, being a good listener is so important to being influential that we had to include it here too. A common trait observed in most believable, credible, and convincing speakers is they are always ready to listen to their addressees and followers. Listen to your followers, business professionals, and loved ones for two major reasons.

First, you need to listen to them to assess how receptive they are to your viewpoint. Secondly, you listen to discover the particular objections they have and that they expect you to resolve. Unless you listen to them, you cannot find out what they want from you and cannot satisfy them. Therefore, always be willing to listen to your loved ones, business associates, and followers if you truly want to come up with winning strategies to persuade them.

Why Managing Stress is Important for Dealing with Difficult People
No one likes dealing with difficult people, but sometimes the task is required. To handle difficult people, you need to be in control of yourself and your stress level first. For people in high-stress jobs such as retail, taking the time to relax and recenter themselves can help provide the emotional energy for dealing

with such individuals. People who do not take the time to refresh and recharge themselves may not be able to handle stressful situations of any kind as well as they otherwise would.

Reactions to Difficult People

The opposite reaction to the dramatic "breaking point" screaming or crying is to shut down. This often happens when people are involved in stressful situations within their own families or in other areas of life where they cannot get away. Shutting down can lead to making unhealthy decisions simply to please the difficult person. This is because making the healthier decision would require fighting and fighting requires energy.

Relieving stress can allow people in these situations to build up their reserves and fight for their own needs to be met. It takes more emotional energy initially but can result in a better situation overall. People who find themselves shutting down may need to remove themselves from the situation until they have recharged their batteries. Then they can fight for their needs.

Offer Satisfaction

Smart persuaders understand they do not need be victorious in every tiny battle. They are willing to sacrifice tiny victories in favor of bigger, better ones. To persuade those around you, do not seek to win every argument. Instead, offer others satisfaction by not battling with them all the time. For instance, you could tell someone he or she is right on trivial issues to boost his or her ego a little. However, when an important issue arises, you stand your ground. Since that individual knows you do not argue 24/7, and that you are more knowledgeable than he or she, they would definitely show their consent to you and do as you say.

Effects of Stress

Stress is a serious issue that has physical, mental and emotional consequences. It can never be entirely avoided because it is a normal reaction to dealing with difficult situations in everyday life. However, it can be dealt with by taking time to relax consciously.

The effects of stress are cumulative to a certain extent. People who work in stressful environments all week are usually much more stressed out on Thursday than on Monday. The weekend provides a chance to rest and recover that the shorter, overnight break between workdays does not offer.

Stress and Emotional Energy

Everyone has had a moment in their lives where they just could not deal with a situation any longer. Usually, the reaction to reaching this point is quite dramatic, involving yelling, tears, or stomping off in a huff. In most cases, it is not the specific situation that caused the person to reach their breaking point, but the amount of emotional energy they had when they got into the situation.

People have longer "fuses" when they are under less stress. Individuals each have their unique ability to deal with emotionally stressful situations, and some are naturally more tolerant of them than others. However, anyone can increase their ability to deal with stressful situations by consciously relieving stress.

Relieving Stress

Ways of relieving stress are unique to individuals. What one person finds lowers their stress level might increase the stress level of another individual. Some common activities that people use for stress relief include physical exertion, social gatherings, quiet time spent with friends and family, creative endeavors and much more. Anything that leaves someone feeling more relaxed when they are finished than when they began can be considered a method of stress relief.

As you deal with difficult people at work or in the home, be aware of your stress levels. If you sense that you are under a lot of stress, remove yourself from the situation. Ask someone else for help to deal with the difficult person so you can reduce your stress and regain your emotional energy. Being calm within yourself is the first step towards successfully dealing with difficult people.

Chapter 28: Avoiding the Office Chaos

Even in the most repetitive jobs, instances where there are office troubles, whether between employees or employer to employees, overall performance is affected. In most companies, a preventive measure is put into action. A monthly or quarterly team outing is budgeted by the company to encourage healthy friendship and camaraderie. Others opt for weekly team meetings, and some choose outright calls for the outrageous display of character while some choose all the mentioned options.

While these may be effective, they are only workable to a certain degree. One of the most important things to take note of is missing from the picture: Competition. The most common reason for the major office fights or troubles often stems from competition. Although competition is also one of the factors of a healthy working condition, a very high level becomes unhealthy for all involved.

Take for example one case. Person 1, who worked for the company three years, got promoted to team manager. Person 2 who also worked for the company for three years, got assigned to work under Person 1 along with Person 3. Person 2 somewhat respects that Person 1 got promoted ahead of her, but she is aiming for the next slot.

However, she meets Person 3, who only worked for the company a good six months. She is astounded to see that Person 3 is very good at her job. She senses that Person 3 may be considered for promotion too. Thus, between the two, there is an unhealthy level of competition especially since Person 1 gives more attention and credit to Person 3. Being the direct boss of Person 2, she needs to find a way to get recognized, but Person 3 has monopolized the picture. Person 3 senses the rift between Person 1 and 2 and subconsciously or consciously takes advantage of it to score more points from Person 1. The whole picture becomes a reflection of Junior High. Not only does this affect the three of them, but it also reflects badly on the higher office.

The moment you sense something brewing after giving someone a promotion, listen very closely and keep your ears to the ground. In most cases, this can be fixed by leveling out the playing field. Promotion and achievement should not be based on the relationship one has with the direct boss but should be on sound working performance, ethics, and positive attitudes.

However, if cases are too severe, all parties involved should be called into a meeting. Then go from there. Addressing the issue as soon as possible is the key to its reconciliation. If you put it off and hope it will be resolved by itself, you are making a mistake. Intervention is needed in extreme cases especially when it already concerns badmouthing and dangerously sensitive office gossip.

Some of the most recognized managers of the biggest firms say that banking on teamwork rather than on solitary achievements not only prevents an unhealthy level of competition but also encourages good working values. Others also attest to painting clear requirements for promotion helps not only put a lid on office squabbles, but it also pushes people to give exactly what the company needs from its people. Other managers choose a more direct approach to this. They say that by implementing a strict no-tolerance policy for office fights is the key.

Misunderstandings in the office is a reality but to have ones that push employees to resort to insensitive behavior or outright shameful words are not. How a manger chooses to handle these is his or her choice; however, it is the business of everyone to ensure office peace. Common courtesy and respect are few of the factors for a solid foundation. Sound management from the higher office helps greatly and laying out an office environment that reflects order and working conditions that encourages teamwork is crucial.

Conclusion

Effective communication is essential in any workplace. When a company has people who practice effective communication skills, working relationships are better, and productivity is higher. Employees tend to respect leaders who can communicate well with their subordinates, and people in middle management appreciate subordinates who can effectively communicate their concerns.

EFFECTIVE COMMUNICATION IN THE WORKPLACE

With the existence of effective communication in the workplace, hostile working environments are avoided. Colleagues gain respect for each other, and interactions with bosses, subordinates or colleagues become pleasant and enjoyable. This contributes to the happiness of employees with their jobs and the company that they work for. Believe it or not, employees tend to value their happiness in the workplace more than their salary because, although money is important for all employees, happiness in their jobs and workplaces is deemed more essential.

The importance of effective communication in the workplace cannot be stressed enough. It is one of the critical determinants that can make or break any business, and is vital to the success of any organization. In fact, many business relationships are impaired because of poor communication, and misinterpretation of facts often makes everything worse.

CPSIA information can be obtained
at www.ICGtesting.com
Printed in the USA
LVHW010024270719
625576LV00001B/78/P

9 781092 221221